香港國際詩歌之夜 2017
INTERNATIONAL POETRY NIGHTS IN HONG KONG

《古老的敵意》

封面影像：北島
封面設計：麥安

國際統一書號（ISBN）：978-988-237-030-2

出版：中文大學出版社
香港 新界 沙田・香港中文大學
傳真：+852 2603 7355
電郵：cup@cuhk.edu.hk
網址：www.chineseupress.com

Ancient Enmity

Cover Image: Bei Dao
Cover Design: Ann Mak

ISBN: 978-988-237-030-2

Published by The Chinese University Press
The Chinese University of Hong Kong
Sha Tin, N.T., Hong Kong
Fax: +852 2603 7355
E-mail: cup@cuhk.edu.hk
Website: www.chineseupress.com

Printed in Hong Kong

古老的敵意

ANCIENT ENMITY

編輯	**Editors**
北島	**Bei Dao**
柯夏智	**Lucas Klein**
宋子江	**Chris Song**

馬蘭・阿勒瑪斯麗 敘利亞	**Maram al-MASRI** Syria
嘉貝巴・巴德倫 南非	**Gabeba BADEROON** South Africa
哈維爾・貝略 智利	**Javier BELLO** Chile
約翰・伯恩塞 英國	**John BURNSIDE** United Kingdom
努諾・朱迪斯 葡萄牙	**Nuno JÚDICE** Portugal
林舜玲 香港	**Agnes S. L. LAM** Hong Kong
瑟梅茲定・梅赫梅迪維奇 波斯尼亞	**Semezdin MEHMEDINOVIĆ** Bosnia
喬治・澤提斯 英國	**George SZIRTES** United Kingdom
馬克・卓狄尼 澳洲	**Mark TREDINNICK** Australia
崔健 中國大陸	**CUI Jian** Mainland China
周耀輝 香港	**CHOW Yiu Fai** Hong Kong
傑閎・格庵 法國	**Jérôme GAME** France
查爾斯・伯恩斯坦 美國	**Charles BERNSTEIN** USA
文貞姬 南韓	**MOON Chung-hee** South Korea
德米特里・維傑尼亞賓 俄羅斯	**Dmitry VEDENYAPIN** Russia
哈里斯・武拉維亞諾斯 希臘	**Haris VLAVIANOS** Greece
洛爾娜・克羅齊 加拿大	**Lorna CROZIER** Canada
悠莉亞・費多奇克 波蘭	**Julia FIEDORCZUK** Poland
平田俊子 日本	**HIRATA Toshiko** Japan
馬卓爾・傑克遜 美國	**Major JACKSON** USA
安雅・烏德勒 德國	**Anja UTLER** Germany
陳滅 香港	**CHAN Chi Tak** Hong Kong
陳東東 中國大陸	**CHEN Dongdong** Mainland China
陳先發 中國大陸	**CHEN Xianfa** Mainland China

古老的敵意——
香港國際詩歌之夜 2017代序

奧地利詩人里爾克（Rainer Maria Rilke）在《安魂曲》中寫下這樣的詩句：「因為生活和偉大的作品之間 / 總存在某種古老的敵意」。對我來説，這詩句就像激盪而持久的迴聲。無論對於詩還是詩人，我們敢於不斷追問，尤其在一個異質與同構抗衡的全球化時代，一個巨大變革的時代，一個沉淪而喧囂的世代，在詩歌的寫作中，是否仍舊存在著某種古老的法則？

在生活與詩歌之間充滿著古老的敵意，我認為，那是因為苦難是詩歌的源泉，也是詩歌的原動力，是生活的苦難和壓迫讓詩歌超越了歷史、民族、宗教、意識形態，甚至語言的邊界。試問，為甚麼中產階級生活方式不可能產生偉大的作品？為甚麼體制中的詩歌創作課不可能「製造」偉大的作品？為甚麼人工智慧與機器人寫作不可能「發明」偉大的作品？

香港國際詩歌之夜2017 的主題是「古老的敵意」。

2009 年11 月，我們創辦了首屆香港國際詩歌之夜，這是第五屆的「詩歌事件」。幸運的是，來自各語種的國際詩人聚在一起，從全世界到亞洲，從香港到大陸，包括武漢、南京、杭州、廈門和廣州的五個城市。特別説明的是，自從2011 年創辦起，我們為每位應邀詩人正式出版雙語或三語的個人詩集，這是迄今為止所有國際詩歌節的出版創舉。

是詩歌洩露天機的時候了
是時候了

北島
2017年7月18日於香港

Ancient Enmity—
International Poetry Nights in Hong Kong 2017

Denn irgendwo ist eine alte Feindschaft / zwischen dem Leben und der großen Arbeit. "For somewhere there is an ancient enmity / between our daily life and the great work," wrote the Austrian poet Rainer Maria Rilke, in one of his "Requiem" poems (Stephen Mitchell, trans.). For me, this line has always echoed with a persistent surge. Whether of the poem or of the poet, it is time to ask—particularly in our globalized era, with its heterogeneity in contention with isomorphism, with all its upheavals, its clamour and its lapses—whether or what ancient principles still exist in our poetry.

For there is an ancient enmity between life and poetry—because, I believe, hardship is the wellspring of poetry, its first motivating force, though it is also the hardships and oppressions of life that allow for poetry to transcend the bounds of history, nationality, religion, ideology, even of language. Why does the middle class lifestyle have such difficulty creating great work? Why is it so rare for great work to be "created" in institutionalized creative writing workshops? Why can't great work be "invented" by robots and Artificial Intelligence?

The theme for the 2017 International Poetry Nights in Hong Kong is *Ancient Enmity*.

In November 2009, we hosted the first International Poetry Nights in Hong Kong, making this now our fifth "poetry event." And now, we are not only able to bring poets to Asia from around the world, but then on from Hong Kong to five cities in the mainland, namely Wuhan, Nanjing, Hangzhou, Xiamen, and Guangzhou. And this is on top of our having published, since 2011, the work of all our invited poets in bi- or trilingual editions—the only such publication program to date of any international poetry festival.

> It's time that poetry revealed the heavenly secrets
> It's time

Bei Dao

18 July, 2017

(Translated from Chinese by Lucas Klein)

目 錄 Contents

香港國際詩歌之夜 *2017*
INTERNATIONAL POETRY NIGHTS IN HONG KONG

馬蘭・阿勒瑪斯麗（敘利亞），曾於大馬士革修讀英國文學，1982 年移居巴黎，現專事寫作和翻譯。她的詩作廣泛發表於文學雜誌、阿拉伯文詩選以及國際詩選，譯成八種語言在多國傳播。曾獲黎巴嫩文化論壇頒發的阿多尼斯獎（1998）、Città di Calopezzati 詩歌獎（地中海類）、法國文學家協會 Prix d'Automne 獎（2007）。

Maram al-Masri (Syria) moved to Paris in 1982 after studying English literature at Damascus. At present she dedicates herself exclusively to literature and translation. Besides numerous poems published in literary journals, in several Arab anthologies and in various international anthologies, she has published several collections of poems. Thus far her work has been translated into eight languages. Received awards include Adonis Prize of the Lebanese Cultural Forum for the best creative work in Arabic in 1998, Premio Città di Calopezzati for the section Poésie de la Méditerranée, Prix d'Automne 2007 of the Société des gens de lettres.

馬蘭·阿勒瑪斯麗

MARAM AL-MASRI

中文翻譯：唐珺

English translation by Theo Dorgan

بحلا

1

كان على الحب
أن يتمسك بخشبة
أو أن يبني سفينة
لينقذ رعاياه
ولكنه كرحالة متأهب دائم ا
للسفر
كبوط عداء
يفضل الرحيل
تاركا وراءه
الأنهار
والجبال
الأغاني
والأشعار
للبحث عن بدايات جديدة
ونهايات حزينة

2

لم نعد نبكي من أجله
نتركه يذهب
من دون أن نتمسك به
مهددينه بالموت إن لم يبق
نتركه يذهب
بدون أن نصطحبه الى الباب
كضيف عزيز
نراقبه من خلف النافذة
وهو يجرجر حقائبه
ملقيا علينا نظرة من يرغب
أن نهرع
لنسقط تحت قدميه
نتركه يذهب
بدون ضجة
بضعة آهات مكبوتة
بضعة عضات على شفاهنا
وبضعة دمعات مكبوحة
لنليق به نحن الضحايا
وكأننا أصبحنا
مدمنين
هجره

3

في كل مرة نمنحه
ناسيين آلامه الماضية
معتقدين أننا
سننجو به هذه المرة
ه جروحه بالألوان
نرسم عليها زهورا
ونقدمه وكأنه جديد
قد بدأ ينبض للتو
مقسمين
ومصدقين أنفسنا

لأن شعره يبيض

لأن سمعه يلبس القطن

لأن منارة عينيه تخبو

و نوارسه تضيع

لأن الحب يشيخ

ومثلنا

يموت

5

الجلد الذي يتهدل

الحب يرى

الأرداف الثقيلة

الحب يرى

الصدر الهابط

الحب يرى

البطن الممزق

أننا لم نعرف أحاسيس كهذه

من قبل

فرحين أننا قد وجدنا

من

سيتلقفه

من سيحضنه

ومن ربما

سيجرحه

من جديد

4

لأنه لا يفوح دائما

برائحة المسك

لأنه غالبا

لا يكون خفيفا

لأنه أحيانا

يكون متعبا

لأنه ينام فاتحا فمه

كان عمري 81 عشرة عاما
عندما جرحتني
نزفت حتى ظننت أنني
سأموت
قاسمة أنني لن أخوض معركة
أخرى
في كل مرة تأتيني
مبتسما ابتسامتك تلك
واعدا بالجنة والأبد
فأعود بدون خوذة ولا درع
واذا بك تمد لي لسانك
طاعنا ما استطعت
وكأنك تريد حقا
أجلي؟
لا أدري بأي أعجوبة أنجو
ولا بأي أعجوبة أقع في
حلبتك؟
بالرغم من حفظي لدروسك

وتجاعيد الشيخوخة
الحب يرى

يرى
الأسنان المسودة
يرى الجروح
والتشقق

إلا أنه
يغمض عينيه عن كل هذا
مكتفيا
بجماله.

6
انظر انظر
الى كل الجروح
لتي أصبت بها في معاركك
هذا الجرح العميق الغامق

انظر انظر إلى هذا الأخير
ما يزال طريا
ما يزال رطبا
ما يزال ينزف. .
رفقا بي هذه المرة
فكما ترى لم يعد هناك مكان
لجرح آخر
وإن. . .
فاجعله جميلاً.

7

منه ننتظر
كل شيء
وعلى عاتقه نضع
كل الأحمال
هل يشفي من وجع الرأس ؟
هل يرمم العظم؟
هل يداوي القهر؟
منه ننتظر كل شيء
تغيير لون البحر والمحيط
التحليق بدون اجنحة
إيقاف العواصف ،المطر
والنيران؟
لكن؟
هل يشفي الحب
من الحب؟
أه وكأنه قادر حقا على
المعجزات

8

أعرفها مقدماً
أراها آتية لا محالة
متنكرة بوجوه ألفتها
متزينة ما أمكنها
مرددة كلمات حفظتها على
ظهر قلب

بطيئة تأتي أم سريعة

تنسى حتى

أن تنتعل حذاءها.

لها رائحة ألفتها

كرائحة إبطي

وملمس قطة ربتيها في حضني.
أربت على ظَهره اً
أهدئه ا
ألاطفها
أتوسل إليها
أتحايل عليها
أبكي
.أمهلها ولا تمهلني
النهايات
غامضٌ
لبدايات قادمة. .

愛

1.
愛，本應當
抓住一塊木板
或是建造一艘船
來拯救它的子民。
可它像一個隨時準備啟程的
旅行家，
像跑步運動員的鞋，
喜歡出發，
把流水、
高山、
歌謠
與詩
甩在後方，
去追尋全新的開始
和悲傷的結局。

2.
我們不再為他哭泣
我們任憑他離開，
不會像對待貴客那樣
把他送到門口。

我們在窗戶後觀察他，
他拖著行李箱，
回頭瞟我們一眼，

以為我們會奔出來
撲在他腳下
求他留下。

我們任憑他離開，
不吵不鬧，
忍住幾聲嘆息，
咬一咬嘴唇，
強壓幾滴眼淚，
去配合他做個受害者，
好似我們已變得
習慣了
他的遺棄。

3.
一次次地，我們向他付出，
忘記了過去的傷痛，
堅信我們
這一次可以將他拯救。

我們給他的傷口鍍上色彩，
在上面畫鮮花。
我們把看似全新的他重新呈現，
就好像他已煥然一新，
心臟即刻可開始跳動。

我們發誓，
我們説服自己
從未有過這番感受，
欣喜自己找到了
可以緊握的人，
可以依偎的人，
可能再次傷害的人。

4.
因為他不會永遠身散麝香，
因為他總是無法體態輕盈，
因為他有時會筋疲力盡，
因為他張著嘴睡覺，

因為他的頭髮變白，
因為他的耳朵塞著棉花，
因為他雙眸的光亮黯淡，
他海鷗般的鋭眼弱散。

因為愛，變老了，
像我們似的，
它會死去。

5.
鬆垮的皮膚，
愛看得見。

下垂的臀部，
愛看得見。

耷拉的胸脯，
愛看得見。
鬆弛的肚子
和衰老的皺紋，
愛看得見。

愛看得見
發黑的牙齒，
看得見
疤痕和裂口。
只是它視而不見，
知足於其中的美。

6.
看看，看看
所有這些傷
都是我在你的戰爭裏所受。

這道深深的暗疤，
是你對18歲時的我所為。
我流著血，以為自己
即將死去，
發誓自己絕不會再掀起另一場戰爭。

每一次，你又找到我，
帶著那種微笑，
承諾天堂與永恆。

於是我卸下盔甲回歸，
你卻用言語
竭盡所能地刺痛我，
就像你想讓我真的
死去？

我不知道是甚麼奇跡可以拯救我，
是哪門子奇跡讓我落入你的手心？

儘管我牢記著你的教訓，
然而，看看，看看這最近的一道傷口，
仍然新鮮，
仍然濕潤，
仍在流血……
這一次，能不能對我仁慈一些！

你也看見了，
再沒有餘地
可以多添一道傷。
如果一定要……
讓它漂亮些好嗎。

7.

對於他，我們期待
所有事情。
我們在他肩膀上
放置所有的負擔。
他能不能療癒頭痛？
他能不能修復骨折？
他能不能醫治壓迫？

對於他，我們期待所有事情。
變換海洋的顏色，
不帶羽翼的翺翔，
止住風暴、降雨和火焰。

可是，
愛能夠治癒愛嗎？

呵，就像他真有能力創造奇跡似的。

8.

我早就認出她來，
我看著她不可避免地到來，
偽裝成一副副我熟悉的面孔，
她竭盡所能地裝扮自己，
重複著那幾句熟記於心的詞語。
她緩緩地、或是迅速地到來，
甚至忘了穿上自己的鞋。

她散發著我熟悉的味道，
像腋下的體味，
或是懷中撫摸貓咪的味道。
我輕拍她的肩膀，
我安撫她，
我對她溫柔以待，
我向她俯首乞憐，
我欺騙她，
我哭泣，
我給她時間，可她卻不給我。

尾聲。
在她的苦澀裏
有下一次開始的
模糊滋味。

LOVE

I.

Love
should have grabbed a board
to float,
or built an ark
to save its subjects,
but like a traveller always outward bound,
like the shoes of a runner,
it prefers to head on out
leaving behind it
    rivers,
        mountains,
            songs and entreaties,
to search out
new beginnings
and sad endings.

II.

We weep no more for him,
we let him leave
without accompanying him to the door
as one would a cherished guest.

We watch from behind the curtains
as he drags his suitcase slowly behind him
until he glances back at us,
hoping we'll run after him,
fall at his feet,
beg him to stay.

We let him go
without a sound — perhaps
a few stifled sighs
    a bitten lip
        a few tears
to earn being his victims,
as if we were accustomed
to his abandoning us.

III.

Over and over we make the offer,
forgetting old pain,
believing that this time he can be saved.

We hide his wounds with colours,
decorate them with flowers,
we present him
as if he were nine
and was beginning
to beat at time.

We swear,

and we believe ourselves,
that we have never known
such feelings before,
so happy to have found
one who will accept,
one who will cherish
and perhaps one
who will wound
again.

IV.

Because he does not always smell
the rose water,
because often he is not
so light,
because he is sometimes
tired
and sleeps
with his mouth open

Because his head is covered with ashes,
because his ears are covered with cotton,
the pilot of his vision weakens,
and he loses the albatross gaze of his eyes

Because love ages him
and like us
he must die

V.

The skin grown soft,
love sees it.
The buttocks sagging,
love sees it.

The empty breasts,
the slack belly
and the wrinkles of age,
love sees it.

Love sees
the blackened teeth
the scars
the stretch marks
the blemished complexion

but
closes its eyes
satisfied
with its own beauty.

VI.

Look, look
at all the wounds I have received
in your wars.

This wound, deep and dark,
I got it at 18,
the first time you injured me.
I bled until I thought I might die,
swore I would never again
get into a fight.

But every time you return,
smiling that smile,
promising paradise and eternity,

back I come again
without helmet or armour
and you lunge at me with your words,
stabbing as hard as you can,
as if, truly,
you wished me dead.

I do not know by what miracle
I survive,
nor by what miracle
I fall back into your arena.

Look, look,
this one is still fresh,
still bleeding.
Be gentle, this time…

You see,
I cannot bear another wound.
At the very least, do it nicely.

VII.

From him, we expect
everything.
On his shoulders, we can place any weight.
Can he heal diseases?
Can he repair broken bones?
Can he treat rheumatism?

From him we expect
everything:
change the colour of the sea
halt storms in their tracks
extinguish fires…

But,
can love heal love?

Ah, if so
it would be capable of miracles.

VIII.
The end —
I know it before it comes,
I watch it arrive
in its inevitable manner
disguised under faces
become familiar,
repeating words
I have begun to know by heart.

It comes slowly,
or hastily as if
it had forgotten
to put on its shoes.

The end —
it's like stroking the fur
of a cat held in my arms.
I trick, I calm, I pamper, I beseech
to quieten it

but love,
love is not listening.

The end
in its bitterness
has the mysterious taste
of some beginning.

嘉貝巴・巴德倫（南非），詩人、學者。詩集 *The Dream in the Next Body*（2005）是《週日獨立報》和《週日時報》推薦書籍。*A Hundred Silences*（2006）入選2007年約翰內斯堡大學詩歌以及2007年Olive Schreiner獎的決選名單。她的瑞典文詩集 *The Silence Before Speaking* 出版於2008年。另獲有Daimler Chrysler南非詩歌獎，取得 Civitella Ranieri 基金會以及北歐非洲研究所的獎學金，並曾於維瓦特斯蘭大學、斯特倫斯堡高等研究院任駐校作家。現於賓州州立大學任教女性研究、非洲研究等科目，並兼任斯特倫斯堡大學英文客座教授。她的下一本詩集名為*Axis and Revolution*。

Gabeba Baderoon (South Africa) is a poet and scholar. She is the author of three poetry collections, *The Dream in the Next Body* (2005), *The Museum of Ordinary Life* (2005) and *A Hundred Silences* (2006). A selected volume of her poetry translated into Swedish, *The Silence Before Speaking*, was published in 2008. *The Dream in the Next Body* was named a Notable Book by the *Sunday Independent* and was a *Sunday Times* Recommended Book. *A Hundred Silences* was a finalist for the 2007 University of Johannesburg Prize and the 2007 Olive Schreiner Award. Baderoon is the recipient of the Daimler Chrysler Award for South African Poetry, and has held fellowships at the Nordic Africa Institute and Civitella Ranieri Foundation, and Writer's Residencies at the University of Witwatersrand and the Stellenbosch Institute for Advanced Study. She teaches Women's Studies and African Studies at Pennsylvania State University, and is an Extraordinary Professor of English at Stellenbosch University. Baderoon is a member of the editorial board of the African Poetry Book Fund, which publishes new chapbooks and full collections by African poets each year. Her fourth book of poetry, titled *Axis and Revolution*, is forthcoming from Kwela books and Northwestern University Press in 2018.

嘉貝巴 · 巴德倫

GABEBA BADEROON

中文翻譯：維絲

The Pen

Three days before my father died
I lost the silver pen with my name on it,
a birthday gift from my aunt
I'd kept for almost ten years.

That day, supervising students in Khayelitsha
putting up a basketball hoop, I came home
to ask to borrow his tools.
We walked around the garage and I ticked
off the ladder, drill, nails and hammer on my list,
and he suggested I add a hammer and a level.
Somewhere between stacking and loading
the car, I lost my pen without even noticing
it had slipped from my hand.

When I went home late that day,
I negotiated with loss as I always do,
not going back to the garage to look for the pen
in case it wasn't there,
to keep its absence incomplete
so it could come back one day.

In three days
the impossible sequence of death.

I went back
over everything we'd said that day
and the years when we didn't speak
and the reconciliation, almost wordless,
when we walked towards each other with our eyes down
and wept while we hugged.

The night he died
I felt the completeness of loss,
of absence without negotiation,

and yet what was still there,
that moving toward each other,
without looking.

筆

父親死去前三天
我遺失了刻有我名字的銀鋼筆
是阿姨送的生日禮物
已保存了近十年

那天在卡耶列沙城指導學生
架立籃球框，我回家
去找父親借工具
我們在車庫裏徘徊，剔上
列表上的梯子、鑽頭、釘子和錘子
他建議我再帶上一把錘子和一座水平儀
我把工具搬到車上
卻把鋼筆弄丟了，都沒有發現
它從手中溜走了

當天晚了回家
我以慣常的方式處理失去
沒有回車庫裏找
以防它不在車庫裏
我讓失去有所缺失
以便有一天它會回來

三天後
便是死亡
不可能的次序

我回想
那天我們説過的話
還有我們互不説話的日子
和解也幾乎無話可説
我們低著頭走向對方
擁抱，啜泣

他死去的那天晚上
我感到失去的完整
缺席的完整，不容我處理

然而，那裏的仍在
朝向彼此，不望對方的
走著

ID Photos

In the small caravan parked permanently next to the Traffic Department
with the handwritten sign ID Photos Taken Here
its wheels rusted into place
the young old photographer with dreadlocks
and a tired poet's face is shaking his head from side to side
muttering some version of no
just before me a woman in a long black skirt
and black veil unties the loop of fabric knotted
behind her head and her face briefly emerges
the young old photographer sees everything
hundreds of unclaimed photos line the inside
of his caravan the making of identity
interrupted and turned into small sad signs
of something else
we don't look at each other so we look
at the walls at the faces no one came to collect
someone stands and someone offers their seat
exact change
I sit on the plastic bar stool
and he takes my picture with a small digital camera like the one
you take holiday photos with
no tripod except his legs and arms
the background behind me
the faded fawn of the caravan wall
that disappears anyway in the end
why do we all hate our ID photos
hair tucked behind the ears
eyes too wide the moment
our identity, identity is being made.
inside the hall with its plastic chairs
a man ahead of me presses his finger onto the ink blotter
a million index fingers and left thumbs before him
then he leans his chin and forehead against the eye-test machine
tell me what you see the officer says
to clean the ink from his thumb
she gives him a single piece
of toilet paper torn carefully at the perforated line
in the last queue to pay for my temporary license I slide
the four photos my ID book completed form and exact change
into the metal slot under the glass
ma'am put your left thumb on the inkpad and place it inside
the block she watches me sign
in the right place and pastes a strip of sellotape over my name
fixing my identity for six months at least

證照

交通部門旁邊總泊著一部小旅行車
上面有「在此拍攝證照」的手寫標示
車輪已鏽到了地面
年輕的老攝影師傅綁著雷鬼頭
掛著詩人的倦容，邊搖頭
邊含糊説著「不」的某個版本
穿著黑色長裙戴著黑色面紗的女人排在我前面
她解開頭後的布結，露出臉
年輕的老攝影師傅看到一切
車箱裏排列著幾百張
無人認領的照片
中斷了身份的生成
轉變成其他事物的標誌
它們渺小而悲傷
我們不望向對方，所以我們看著
牆上無人領取的臉孔
有人站著，有人讓座
不設找贖
我坐在膠吧椅上
他用一般旅遊用的
輕便數碼相機給我拍照
沒有三腳架，只用他的手和腳
身後的背景
旅行車淡黃牆壁都褪色了
到頭來總會消失的

為甚麼我們都討厭自己的證照
頭髮別到耳後
眼睛在那一刻睜得老大
我們的身份，身份正在生成
在擺滿膠椅的大堂裏
排在前面的男人將手指壓在吸墨器
還有他前面過百萬隻食指和左拇指上
下巴和前額靠在檢測視力的機器上
職員説：告訴我你看見了甚麼
為了抹去手指上的油墨
她小心翼翼按虛線撕下一格廁紙
最後排隊繳交臨時執照的費用時
我在櫃台窗底的錢槽遞上
四張照片、身份證、填妥的表格和應繳的費用
女士，請把您的左拇指放在印台上然後放在
方格內按下，她看著我在正確的位置
簽名然後在我的名字上貼上膠紙
將我的身份固定至少六個月

Poetry for Beginners

In the evening poetry class for beginners
in the community hall during the introductions

a girl looking down behind her hair
and a thick brown coat she doesn't take off

breathes in deep and risking
something says fast

my boyfriend's in prison and I'm here

to find out how to write to him
through the bars

and someone laughs

and she pulls herself back into her coat
and from inside looks past us

and the next week doesn't
come back

and I think of her for years
and what poetry is

I think of her long pause
at the beginning

her silence before
and her silence after

and this is my origin
where poetry is risk, is betrayal

and the memory of the first question
how not to be alone

詩歌入門

在社區會堂裏為夜間的
詩歌入門課作引介時

一位女子低頭看
隔著頭髮和未脱下的啡色大衣

深深吸一口氣，似乎冒著
危險，快快説出

我的男朋友在監獄裏，而我在這裏

是想學會寫信
穿過監獄的鐵窗

有人笑了

她縮回大衣裏
從裏面看我們

第二個星期
她沒有回來

這些年我總想起她
想起詩歌為何物

想起她起初
長長的停頓

沉靜之前
和之後

這是我的原點
此處詩歌是冒險，是背叛

記起當時的第一個問題：
如何才不會孤單

哈維爾・貝略（智利）從馬德里孔普魯騰塞大學獲西語文學博士學位，現任智利大學拉丁美洲及智利文學助理教授。第一本詩集 *La noche venenosa* 出版於1987年，此後詩作得到廣泛的發表、收錄及翻譯。1992年獲任Pablo Neruda基金會成員。曾獲獎項包括 Gabriela Mistral 市政文學獎（1994）、Jaime Gil de Biedma 國際詩歌獎（1998）、Juan Ramón Jiménez 西語美洲詩歌獎（2006）、Pablo Neruda 詩歌獎（2007）等。

Javier Bello (Chile) holds a Ph.D. in Spanish Literature from the Complutense University of Madrid and is now Assistant Professor in Latin American and Chilean Literature at the University of Chile. He published his first book of poems *La noche venenosa* (Concepción, Letra Nueva) in 1987. Since then his poems have been widely published, anthologized and translated. In 1992, he became a fellow of the Pablo Neruda Foundation. His honours include the Gabriela Mistral Municipal Literary Prize (1994), the Jaime Gil de Biedma International Poetry Prize (1998), the Juan Ramón Jiménez Hispanic American Poetry Prize (2006), the Pablo Neruda Award (2007), etc.

哈維爾・貝略

JAVIER BELLO

中文翻譯：胡續冬、袁婧

English translation by Valentino Giannuzi

Modelo Benjamin

Mala señal, el centinela se lava los pies con la jarra del vínculo,
mis labios ya no tienen vergüenza,
las oraciones entran de espaldas al orfelinato con cortes en las rodillas.
Es la hora, cierro los ojos, arrugan largos besos,
las esquelas se ahogan en los almanaques botánicos
con la dura humedad de la entrepierna del bosque.
Despeinados por una mano sin madre
los sauces enloquecen, sin pensar en la tierra
las raíces se hunden, los jueces se arremangan,
la prostituta de carbón moja los sobres, está sola, gotean
pensamientos afilados por la desesperación de las tibias,
el empeine dorado del ladrón entra en las franelas,
cruza el enjambre, zumba cuando levanta los vestidos,
espolvorea ruina en las enaguas.
Mala señal, el aceite de la lámpara durará hasta que cante el gallo,
todavía me queda un poco de saliva,
la lluvia me negará tres veces,
será abandonada descalza al borde de la carretera,
apagará en ella sus deseos, montará en caballos mojados.
La fe está sucia, la soledad está sucia,
el viento analfabeto deletrea sedición en las cartas,
una noche para encontrar refugio, para asolar aldeas,
una luna donde volcar los frascos.
Ellos huelen a pólvora, se arrastran por los muelles,
surten de esperma el navío fantasma,
animales al sol babean los braseros,
el incesto camina con los píes manchados.
Pienso que nunca se abolirá el invierno,
sueño con un caballo, un lecho transparente,
cebo y paraíso, un huevo en el riñón de la fábula.
Puedo alimentar los inmensos silabarios de hueso
con las líneas de mi mano, puedo imitar incluso
la respiración de mi madre.
Cierro los ojos, tiznados celadores vigilan el espejo,
mastican agujeros de nieve, en la frontera supuran sinagogas.
Ponte de pie, ya es hora, me dice una voz poderosa,
tenemos cuentas pendientes, soy el pasado,
soy débil, tengo una cita con Sholem.

本雅明模式

不祥之兆，守衛用相連的罐子洗腳，
我的嘴唇已經沒有了羞恥，
語句背著身進入孤兒院，膝蓋上帶著刀傷。
是時候了，我閉上眼睛，長吻皺縮，
書信溺死在植物學年鑒裏
用森林的胯下難捱的潮濕。
頭髮被一隻沒有母親的手撩亂
柳樹發瘋了，不再想著大地
根須沉沒，法官下定決心，
碳的妓女打濕了信封，她獨自一人
削尖的思想從脛骨的絕望裏滴落，
小偷金色的腳背進入法蘭絨，
有蜂群經過，掀起衣服時嗡嗡作響，
在襯裙上播撒廢墟。
不祥之兆，燈油將會堅持到雄雞高唱，
我仍有一點點唾液，
雨水將要拒絕我三次，
雨將赤腳被拋棄在公路邊上，
它泯滅了欲望，騎上潮濕的馬群。
信念是骯髒的，孤獨是骯髒的，
不識字的風在信中拼讀出嘩變，
一個尋找庇護、摧毀村莊的夜晚，
一輪有很多小瓶子被打翻的月亮。
它們聞起來像火藥，摩擦著碼頭，
提供著精液。幽靈船，
動物們朝著太陽淌口水，火盆，
亂倫以污穢的腳行走。
我認為冬天永遠都不會被廢止，
我夢見一匹馬、一張透明的床，
飼料和天堂，一枚寓言之腎中的蛋。
我可以用的我掌紋來餵養
骨頭裏無限的音節表，我甚至
可以模仿我母親的呼吸。
我閉上眼睛，烏黑的衛兵們守護著鏡子，
咀嚼著雪之孔洞，猶太會堂在邊界上潰爛。
出發吧，是時候了，一個強有力的聲音對我説，
我們還有沒算完的賬，我是過去，
我是虛弱的，我和舒勒姆[1]有約。

1　譯註：這裏的舒勒姆可能只是哥舒姆．舒勒姆（Gershom Scholem），其中Scholem轉寫為西班牙語時變為Sholem。哥舒姆．舒勒姆（1897–1982），二十世紀最重要的猶太神秘主義學者、歷史學家，瓦爾特．本雅明的友人。

Benjamin Model

A bad sign, the sentinel washes his feet with the jar of relation
my lips are shameless,
sentences give their back to the orphanage, their knees severed.
It's time, eyes closed, large kisses wrinkle,
Obituaries drown in the botanical almanacs
with the harsh dampness of the forest's crotch.
Their hair disheveled by a motherless hand
the willow-trees go mad, oblivious of the soil
the roots deepen, the judges roll up their sleeves,
the coal whore dampens the envelopes, alone
thoughts drip, sharpened by the desperation of the tibias,
the burglar's golden insteps fits the flannels,
crosses the swarm of bees, buzzes when he raises the dresses,
sprinkles the petticoats with doom,
A bad sign, the oil in the lamp will last till the cook crows,
I still have a bit of spit,
the rain will thrice deny me,
it will be abandoned at the side of the road, barefoot,
it will quench its desires in it, will ride wet horses.
Faith is stained, solitude is stained,
the illiterate wind spells sedition in the letters,
a night to find refuge, to haunt towns,
a moon in which to pour every jar.
They smell of gunpowder, they crawl by the docks,
they supply the ghost ship with sperm,
basking animals slobber the braziers,
incest walks with tainted feet.
Winter will never be abolished, I think,
I dream of a horse, a transparent bed,
bait and paradise, an egg in the fable's kidney.
I can feed the immense syllabaries of bone
with the lines of my palm, can even imitate
my mother's breathing.
I close my eyes, smutty watchmen guard the mirror,
chewing holes of snow synagogues suppurate on the border.
Stand up, it is time, a powerful voice tells me,
we have unfinished business, I am the past,
I am weak, I have an appointment with Sholem.

de *letrero de albergue*

* * *

Detrás del pensamiento hay un palo quebrado. Un palo que arrastró la corriente hasta los pies de la cama. Los vidrios son retratos donde los muertos preguntan por sus manos. Detrás de los espejos hay otra plantación erizada. Hilos de fuego que pulsan las muchachas en coma. Un túnel lleno de semanas. Un túnel quiere decir túnel. Lo que quiere decir cáncer. Invernadero y sed. Bolsa marsupial. Leche de oído. El hígado habla en las esquinas. Un vino lleno de números. Un saco de hojas secas detrás de la mirada. Una bolsa de té. Un ataúd repleto de ramas. Debajo de la edad están los años muertos. Debajo de la luz los prismas resucitados. Un niño carga un puente que carga a otro niño que no carga nada. El vacío es una enfermedad a la sangre. Decanta como el óxido en las redes de pesca. En todos los armarios hay espectros. En los cajones manos desconsoladas. Las paredes las ha rayado nadie. El otoño tiene muchos nombres. Detrás del pensamiento yo sé quien es nadie.

* * *

El excesivo equipaje no deja caminar a la sombra. El vagabundo visita la provincia otoñal, el silabario de tiza de las cantinas donde aprenden a leer los fantasmas. La sombra, por supuesto, es esta voz. Por supuesto, esta mano que esconde un alfiler de gancho en el bolsillo de un muchacho dormido. Un muchacho desnudo sobre la pelusa fértil del bosque. Llueve debajo de las mantas. Llueve una lluvia interminable. La sombra cuenta los días con los dedos. Un bote colorado cruza un río verde. La sombra se embarca, orina en la vertiente helada. Hace sombra, humo hace. Humo contra el tamiz de la luz. Así el día se abre, se corona de agua. De cadáver y viñedo de mar se fecunda la noche. Canta la voz su hueco sin voz. Los insectos se alían contra el miedo. Cruje el grillo de los espinos rojos. La luna hace lo que puede en abril. Le lima las uñas a los perros. La nariz se mece entre las ramas. Aletea como pez en la arena. Todo podría continuar así. La sombra me toma de la mano. Me lleva a un jardín con miedo. A un parque con estatuas vendadas. Dónde iremos mi poema y yo. La sombra sabe de qué hablo, del fuego que salta entre los álamos. La voz flota en el lago de caucho. Se escucha en los pozos sellados. Qué dice el caminante que visitó los puertos. Qué oyó de la boca del mar y sus milicianos húmedos. Lo que oyó apoyado en sus hondas rodillas, con la lengua en los odres. Lo que anduvo, lo que amó, el agua que dejó correr. Todas las cosas. La aldea y sus ciervos helados. El río con su pata de alma de molino viejo. La estrechez de la sombra. La más delgada voz. En fin, la voz.

* * *

> ¿Quién oyó?
> ¿Quién oyó?
> ¿Quién ha visto lo que yo?
> —Góngora

dónde está la oreja noche.
dónde está la noche oír y no temer.
para qué tiene oreja la noche.
oír qué. queda batalla.
los collares exaltan un ave del montón y ese pájaro sufre.
sufre su cáñamo azul.
su madera de lince.
su páramo.
su puerta.
quien se marcha no deja decir.
su minuto no dice.
oigo el pie del ladrón.
qué se lleva pequeño asustado. pequeño quemado. lo lleva al sol. al mar. lo lleva al precipicio. un liquen santo. un manojo húmedo que da de comer. lámpara da de comer. artefacto de espuma y demonio no dice. para qué va a decir el pulmón. lo llena de rizos. lo riza su madre. yo llegaré hasta aquí. dormido seré el ilegible. cargo piedras de río. oreja de piedra. tuve sed y permiso de la sed. tuve sed y dominio. no la garganta. me sigue por la cuesta. algo me va diciendo. vi los pobres muertos. lejos de lavativa y vecindad. lejos de nadie. la cajita feroz. un párpado nupcial. otro de lepra. la noche se degüella de pie. cascabeles. circo de pus. muebles con tetas. a dónde va la oreja. la dejo de alguacil. la alejo entre sus pasos. como gran alacrán. como anzuelo que como. mi ojo sin ciudad. mi pez sin candelabro. oír y no temer. llevo la cuenta

* * *

no es traducible el hueso, lo que viene después del hueso, paloma sometida dentro del cadáver. la mano donde cabe la mano que hizo todo el fuego, la imagen cuando cae en la sombra adivina la crueldad de los restos, pianos elementales contra el objeto norte, contra el fragmento alzado. los dedos muertos crecen en el bosque, el árbol acaba de parir piedra a la espalda, té de espinas en la cabeza del pastor, pozo allegado al misterio. no puedo traducir el señuelo, el hocico de los largos inviernos, esta lluvia que acorta las distancias, moja el hospicio de los muertos. un rostro no es traducible, el horizonte no es traducible, tu rostro verónica en las manos no dice nada al humo en el camino, no habla entre los sexos espontáneos. hay un suicidio, hay algo entre las piernas. una boca en el agua me sonríe, un alto filamento abre las puertas, pero muestra los dientes y se Cierra

選自《旅館招牌》

* * *

思想的後面有一根斷裂的棍子。一根把流體拖拽到床腳的棍子。玻璃是畫像，在其中死者索求他們的手。鏡子的後面是另外一片支楞著的植被。昏迷中的姑娘們彈撥著火焰的絲線。一條滿是星期的隧道。這裏的隧道説的就是隧道。也就是説癌症。溫室和乾渴。有袋動物的育兒袋。聽覺之奶。肝臟在那些角落裏説話。一瓶滿是數字的酒。視線後面的一袋枯葉。一包茶。一副裝滿樹枝的棺材。年齡的下面是死去的年份。光亮之下，棱鏡復活。一個孩子扛著一座橋，那橋扛著另一個孩子，那孩子沒扛任何東西。空是一種深入血液的病。像漁網上的氧化物一樣脱落。所有的衣櫃裏都有幽靈。抽屜裏難以慰藉的手。無人劃過的牆。秋天有很多名字。在思想的後面，我知道誰是無人。

* * *

過重的行李讓影子無法行走。流浪漢造訪秋之外省，小酒館裏粉筆的音節表，幽靈在這裏學習誦讀。那個影子，毫無疑問，就是這聲音。毫無疑問，這隻手把一根別針藏在熟睡的男孩的口袋裏。森林肥沃的絨毛上一個赤裸的男孩。雨下在層疊的毯子下。下著冗長的雨。那個影子用手指數著日子。彩船穿過綠色的河。影子上船，在冰凍的小溪上小便。有陰影，有煙。煙塵撲向光線的篩子。如是，白晝開啟，以水加冕。以屍體、以海上葡萄園滋養夜晚。聲音歌唱它沒有聲音的洞。蟲子們聯合起來對抗恐懼。長著紅刺的蟋蟀沙沙作響。月亮做著它在四月裏能做的事情。它打磨著狗群的指甲。鼻子在樹枝間晃動。像沙灘上的魚一樣擺尾。也許一切都可以像這樣繼續下去。影子拉起我的手。它怯生生地把我帶到一座花園。一個裏面雕像都纏著繃帶的園子。我的詩和我將去往何方。影子知道我說的是甚麼，楊樹之間躍動的火。那聲音在橡膠湖上漂浮。在每一個封口的井裏都能聽見。來到港口的那個路人說著甚麼。從大海和它潮濕的義勇軍的口中能聽到甚麼。舌頭在酒囊中、膝蓋深陷時所聽到的。走過的，愛過的，任其奔流的水。萬事萬物。村莊和它冰凍的小鹿們。河流，它有著老磨坊的靈魂長出的爪子。影子的逼仄。最消瘦的聲音。總之，聲音。

* * *

誰聽到了？
誰聽到了？
誰看到了我之所見？
——貢戈拉

夜晚之耳在哪裏。傾聽而毫無畏懼的夜在哪裏。夜晚緣何有耳。聽到了甚麼。留下戰爭。頸鏈令一隻平凡的鳥興奮不已，亦使它遭受折磨。它藍色的麻布遭受折磨。它的猞猁之木。它的荒野。它的門。出發的人緘口不語。它分秒不說。我聽到小偷的腳。這受驚嚇的小傢伙帶走了甚麼。被火燒的小傢伙。他把它帶到太陽。帶到大海。他把它帶到懸崖。一片神聖的地衣。提供食物的一小把潮濕。燈盞餵食。泡沫和魔鬼構成的器械不說話。肺為何說話。讓它充滿彎曲。它媽媽卷著它。我將到達這裏。熟睡的我難以辨認。我背負著河裏的石頭。石頭之耳。我曾渴過，且曾被允許渴。我曾渴過，且曾有所掌控。不是喉嚨。它沿著斜坡跟隨我。某物對我慢慢講述。我曾見過那些可憐的死者。遠離灌腸藥和鄰里。遠離無人。凶猛的小棺材。一片婚禮的眼瞼。另一片是麻風病的。夜晚自斷其足。鈴鐺。膿水馬戲團。有乳房的家具。耳朵去往何方。我將它交付給巡警。我任其漸行漸遠。像巨大的蝎子。像我咬住的魚鈎。沒有城市的我的眼。沒有大燭台的我的魚。傾聽而毫無畏懼。我數著。

* * *

骨頭是不可譯的，骨頭之後到來的東西，屍體之中臣服的鴿子。手裏有另一隻點燃所有火的手，那畫面墜入陰影之時，猜想著殘骸上的殘忍，那些初級的鋼琴緊靠著北方的目標，緊靠著豎起的碎片。死去的指頭在森林中生長，那棵樹剛剛在身後產下了石頭，牧羊人頭上帶刺的茶，瀕臨秘境的井。我不能翻譯誘餌，漫長冬日的獸嘴，這場縮短了距離的雨，潤濕了死者的收容所。一張面孔是不可譯的，地平線是不可譯的，手中維羅妮卡布巾上你的面孔在路上甚麼也沒有對煙霧説，在突如其來的性之間不言不語。有人自殺，雙腿之間有某物。水中的一張嘴朝著我笑，一根高處的絲線打開了那些門，但展示出牙齒隨即關閉。

from *letrero de albergue*

* * *

Behind thought lies a broken stick. A stick washed by the tide to the foot of the bed. Glasses are portraits where the dead ask after their hands. Behind the mirrors there is another bristling plantation. Girls in a coma thumbing threads of flames. A tunnel full of weeks. A tunnel means a tunnel. Which means cancer. Greenhouse and thirst. Marsupial pouch. Earmilk. The liver mutters in a corner. A wine full of numbers. A bag of dry leaves behind the eyes. A tea-bags. A coffin filled with shrubbery. Under one's age, the dead years. Under the light, the prisms reborn. A boy carries a bridge which carries another boy who carries nothings. Emptiness is a blood condition. It pours down as rust into fishnets. There are ghosts in every closet. Drawers in crestfallen hands. Nobody has streaked the walls. Autumn has many names. Behind thought, I know who no one is.

* * *

The extra luggage does not let the shadow walk. The wanderer visits the autumnal province, the chalk-drawn syllabary of bars where ghosts learn to read. The shadow, of course, is this voice. This hand, of course, which hides a safety pin in the pockets of a sleeping boy. A naked boy on the fertile fuzz of the forest. It rains under the sheets. A never-ending rain. The shadow courts the days on its fingers. A red boat crosses a green river. The shadow gets into it, urinates on the frozen watershed. Casts a shadow, yields smoke. Smoke against the sieve of light. The day opens, water-crowned. Night is fecundated by corpses and sea-vineyards. The voice sings its voiceless void. Insects join against fear. The cricket creaks on the rad hawthorns. The April moon does what it can. It files down the dogs' fingernails. The nose balances on the branches. It slithers like a fish in sand. Everything could go on like this. The shadow grabs me by the hand. Leads me to a garden, fearfully. To a park of blindfolded statues. My poem and I, where are we heading. The shadow knows what I'm talking about, about the fire bouncing among the elms. The voice floats on a lake of rubber. It is heard on the sealed wells. What says the wanderer who visited the harbours. What did he hear from the lips of the sea and its damp militia. What he heard leaning on his deep knees, his tongue on the wineskins. What he walked, what he loved, the water he let flow. Every single thing. The town and its frozen dears. The river and its feet like the soul of an old mill. The narrowness of the shadow. The thinnest voice. In sum, the voice.

* * *

> ¿Quién oyó?
> ¿Quién oyó?
> ¿Quién ha visto lo que yo?
> —Góngora

where is the ear of the night. where is the night hearing and not fearing. why does the night have an ear. hearing what. battle remains. the necklaces exalt a bird from the lot and that bird suffers. its suffers its blue hemp. its lynx wood. its moor. its door. the one who leaves does not allow saying. its minute does not say. I hear the robber's foot. what it takes small scared. small burnt. takes it to the sun. to the sea. take it to the abyss. a sacred lichen. a wet handful that nurtures. lamp that nurtures. artifact of foam and demon who doesn't say. why would it say lung. it fills it with curls. It's mother curls it. I will get this far. asleep I would be the illegible. I carry river stone. ears of stone. I was thirsty and the thirst gave me leave. I was thirsty and dominion. not the throat. it follows me through the hill. something it tells me. I saw the dead, the poor dead. far from burdens and immediacy. far from no one. the fierce box. a nuptial eyelid. an eyelid of leprosy. night is beheaded on its feet. jingle-bells. circus of pus. furniture with breasts. where does the ear go. I leave it as a sheriff. I distance it among its steps. as a great scorpion. as a bait I eat. my city-less eye. my fish without candelabrum. to hear and not to hear. I'm the record keeper.

* * *

the bone is untranslatable, or what comes after the bone, defected dove within the corpse. The hand which keeps the hand that created all the fire, the image when it falls over the shadow guesses the cruelty of the remains, elemental pianos against the north object, against the raised fragment. dead fingers grow in the forest, the tree has just engendered a stone for the back, tea of thorns on the head of a shepherd, a well neighbouring the mystery. I can't translate the bait, the snout of long winters, the rain shortening distances, drenches the hospices of the dead. a face is not translatable, the horizon is not translatable, your face veronica on your palms says nothing to the smoke on the road, it doesn't talk among spontaneous sexes. there's a suicide, there's something between the legs. a mouth in the winter smiles at me, a high thread opens the doors, but only shows its teeth and closes.

de *Estación noche*

* * *

De frente, sin ciudad, el tren se enmascara
se conduce el solitario, la continuidad no duele
si están todos los brazos levantados
Lo entiendo: dentro de un sol el ejercicio permuta la muerte
por la mirilla destinada a oscurecer
Los focos se disuelven en el patio
hacia su libertad, su desastre: abejas
visillos, estandartes de toda lumbre, oro, relación

El solitario es la pregunta que falta entre una mano y otra
el acento del menesteroso relumbra aunque llueva
en los lugares oscuros con la brevedad de la muerte
su cara de espejismo, su fulgor
se parece a una pradera que despierta
entra en trance, un libro que no para de caer

Padre de nada, entre linternas, entre hijos que se arrugan
para ir a hablar contigo crucé el río
que desde lejos miente en su trabajo de trepidar
He tendido en el puente el arco de mi soledad
oh frente siempre acompañada te he mirado
los labios matutinos, la miel de los muertos
que gotea en la niebla sobre el pez de las horas mojadas

Me resulta difícil desconocer la luz
como si esto nunca hubiera sucedido
Preguntas mal hechas ante el carbón de los rieles
En los peores días, con su murmullo a cuestas
las cosas se hunden afiladas, dejan de existir

* * *

El objeto más hermoso es ese seno izquierdo de la hermana de Shakespeare
traspasado por la bala del orfanatorio
ese seno entreabierto por el cable dentado de los incorruptos
por la huella siniestra de los vínculos, acueductos que ceden, que invaden
por esa bala que tiñen, sonrisa de la muerte y las preguntas
cerrojo de los orfanatorios que ladran ante ese seno enfermo
una mano trenzada que no deja de trenzarse en la nada
después de la muerte la nueva medida de los dedos
el instrumento espera la mitad del sueño que nadie elabora
abejas inamovibles a la orilla de un mar que no alcanza
grave invernadero, piedras podridas donde decanta la cabellera del fondo
Miro las poblaciones quemadas por el vuelo de los primeros descalzos
los últimos gritos marinos que nadie defiende,
    la mitad sin hablar
El objeto más hermoso es ese hemisferio que pierde su llave
el niño y el engendro pintan una escena en los vidrios sagrados
gira el vértigo por los caminos, resopla el fantasma del cuerpo
el cuerpo ulcerado del gran orificio magnético
Yo he visto mi cuerpo, mitad sin mitad, su reino no es de este mundo
su sexo no es de este mundo, la hermana del huevo no es de este mundo

選自《夜間車站》

* * *

前方，沒有城市，火車戴上面具
孤獨者自行運轉，持續性不疼痛
如果所有的手臂都高舉起來的話
我知道：在一個太陽之中練習置換了死亡
通過朝向暗處的窺視孔
焦點在庭院中消融
向著它的自由、它的災難：蜂群、
紗簾、所有火焰的旗幟、黃金、關聯

孤獨者是一隻手和另一隻手之間缺失的問題
貧窮者的口音光芒四射，儘管它會
和死亡的短暫性一起滴落在幽暗的地帶
它幻影般的臉、它的光亮
像一片蘇醒的草原
像一本不停地墜落的書，進入危難之中

虛無之父，在提燈之間，在皺縮的孩子之間
為了去和你交談我穿過了
在它猶疑的勞作中一路撒謊而來的河流
我把我孤獨的拱在橋上鋪開
哦，常被伴隨的額頭，我看見了你
早晨的嘴唇，死者的蜜
滴落在潮濕時辰的魚之上的霧中

我很難無視這光
就好像這一切從未發生過
鐵軌的碳前糟糕的問題
在最壞的日子裏，帶著脊背上的碎語
那些事物變得細小並沉沒下去，不復存在

* * *

最美的事物是莎士比亞的妹妹左邊的那個乳房
被孤兒院的子彈打穿
被純潔者的鋸齒纜繩
被傳輸著、入侵著的導管連接而成的不祥印痕
被染了色的子彈、死亡和問題的微笑微微打開的那個乳房
在那有病的乳房前狂吠的孤兒院的門閂
一隻不停地扭動在空無之中的扭曲的手
死亡之後，指頭的全新尺度
工具等待著無人編製之夢的一半
莊重的溫室無法抵達的海岸邊上
靜止的蜂群，深處的頭髮在其中傾瀉的腐爛石頭
我看見被焚燒的人群，一半無語，被最初的赤腳的飛行所焚燒
最後的海之呼喊無人看護
最美的事物是丟失了鑰匙的那個半球體
孩子和胎兒在神聖的玻璃上畫出一幕場景
眩暈在路上旋轉，身體的幽靈大聲喘息
有著巨大的磁性創口的軀體
我見過我的身軀，有一半沒一半，它的王國不屬於這個世界
它的性不屬於這個世界，蛋的妹妹不屬於這個世界

from *Estación noche*

***

Straight ahead, without a city, the train wears a mask
drives itself, alone, continuity does not hurt
if all the arms are raised
I understand: within a sun exercise exchanges death
through the eyehole destined to darken
The light-bulbs dissolve on the patio
towards their freedom, their doom: bees
blinds, banner of every light, gold, narrative

The lonely is the question missing between one hand and the other
the accent of the wretched glows even though it may rain
in the dark places with the brevity of death
its face of mirage, its shimmering
like a prairie that wakes
in a trance, a book that keep falling

Father of nothingness, among lanterns, among wrinkling sons
in order to talk to you, I crossed the river
which tells lies from afar in its hesitating task
The bridge is hung with the arc of my solitude
oh, forehead, I have always seen you in company
the morning lips, the honey of the dead
dripping in the fog over the fish of damp hours

It's hard for me to not know the light
as if this had never happened
Ill-formulated questions before the coal of the railway
on the worst days, carrying its whispering
things sink, sharpened, they cease to exist.

* * *

The most beautiful object is Shakespeare's sister's left breast
pierced by the bullet from the orphanage
the breast half open by the serrated cable of the incorruptibles
by the sinister track of the relations, aqueducts that fail, the invade
by that bullet they dye, smile of death and the questions
locks of orphanages that bark facing that sick breast
an interlaced hand which does not cease to interlace to nothingness
after death the new measure for fingers
the instrument awaits for the other half of the dream which no one produces
unmovable bees on the shores of an unattainable sea
serious greenhouse, rotten stones where the deep hair flows
I see the population burnt by the flight of the early barefoot
the final marine screams that no one stands for, the speechless half
The most beautiful object is that hemisphere which loses its key
the boy and the monster paint a scene in the sacred stained glass
vertigo turns through the roads, the ghost of the body is blowing
the ulcer-ridden body of the great magnetic orifice
I have seen my body, halfless half, its kingdom is not of this world
its sex is not of this world, the egg's sister is not of this world

約翰・伯恩塞（英國），聖安德魯斯大學創意寫作教授，蘇格蘭重要的當代作家，著有多本詩集、小說集和回憶錄。他的第一本詩集 *The Hoop*（1988）獲蘇格蘭藝術委員會書獎，*Feast Days*（1992）獲 Geoffrey Faber 紀念獎，*The Asylum Dance*（2000）獲 Whitbread 詩歌獎。2012 年憑詩集 *Black Cat Bone* 獲 T. S. Eliot 詩歌獎和 Forward 年度詩集獎。2017 年發表小說 *Ashland & Vine* 及詩集 *Still Life with Feeding Snake*。

John Burnside (United Kingdom) is Professor in Creative Writing at St Andrews University. His prizewinning poetry collections include *The Hoop* (1988), winner of Scottish Arts Council Book Award, *Feast Days* (1992), winner of the Geoffrey Faber Memorial Prize, and *The Asylum Dance* (2000), winner of the Whitbread Poetry Award. His *Black Cat Bone* won both the Forward Poetry Prize (Best Poetry Collection of the Year) and the T. S. Eliot prizes in 2012. His most recent novel, *Ashland & Vine* (Jonathan Cape, 2017) was published alongside a new collection of poetry, *Still Life with Feeding Snake*, in February 2017.

約翰 · 伯恩塞

JOHN BURNSIDE

中文翻譯：鄭政恒

III Self Portrait in 1979

Whatever the misery, he could not regain
contentment with a world which, once
doubted, became absurd.
—Sinclair Lewis

As if he had a Babylon to lose
or years of mother love to wash away,

he makes believe the skin is fanciful,
a ripening delayed just long enough

to memorise the rain;
and though it cannot last, this narrative

of curdled sheets
and methamphetamine

is all the Boy's Own Life he's ever known
that doesn't stink of aspic or fair play.

No one is there to tell him that the heart
is mostly grease and muscle, home

more rented room than permanent abode;
and summer comes too early, dry leaves

powdered in the dust, the cesspits
crusting in the backstreets, clogged with hair.

Away, on the thin edge of town,
stunned animals go down into a fold

of blood and night to make the burger meat
the tourists fatten on, obese and white,

but slick with sitcom sass.
At daybreak, rum and perfume on his lips,

he dips from sleep to waking, sleep
to sleep, until the train slows on a stretch

of brush and tinder, light
and fog streaked through the grass and all

the usual rubbish, chunks of bottle glass,
old beer cans, spills of newsprint, plastic scrim.

For a moment, under his breath, he sings,
there must be some way out —a memory

of soft scald at the bone, and all at once
he wants the same again, same words, same gaze,

the same good story from the same old song
—*there must be some way out* and, after all,

he knows they have people for this
in the great beyond,

experts in luring the out—patient back to his cell,
and lighting a lamp, the city receding at last

while the key in the lock turns so softly,
he has to believe

he will know what he loved all along,
when it comes to the Rapture.

IV Indelible

I should like De Haan to see a study of mine of a lighted candle and two novels (one yellow, the other pink) lying on an empty chair (really Gauguin's chair), a size 30 canvas, in red and green. I have just been working again today on its pendant, my own empty chair, a white deal chair with a pipe and a tobacco pouch. In these two studies, as in others, I have tried for an effect of light by means of clear colour, probably De Haan would understand exactly what I was trying to get if you read to him what I have written on the subject.

—Vincent van Gogh
Letter to Theo, 17th January 1889

Forty years dead, my mother is dicing a heart
at the kitchen table.
Rain at the door, but soon it will turn to sleet
and, later, from here to the woods
there will be snow.

In that house, the windows would cloud
in minutes,
and all weekend we could have been alone,
the rest of the town abandoned, as far as we knew,
nothing beyond the garden, no church, no people.

Now she is here, in my kitchen, dicing a heart:
a saucer of salt at her elbow, a handful of flour
sprinkled across the table, the radio on,

she works as she always did, absorbed in the task,
the chef's-knife catching the light of this winter's noon.

I have never believed in ghosts, and I've no great wish
to see my dead again,
but how could I not respect what refuses to fade,
like the blur in the paint where a hand or a porcelain bowl
conceals the *pentimento* of a tethered

songbird, or that poppy-coloured stain
emerging, once more,
when we whitewash the scullery wall?
How could the boy in my shoes quite disbelieve
what they told me about

the friend of a friend of a friend
who witnessed a light that nobody could explain,
a lucency over the pond where, decades ago,
the baker's son fell through the ice, in the paraffin blue
of Hogmanay, when nobody was watching?

I remember us stopping one day, in a sudden fog,
out for a Sunday walk, the trees
a held breath in the sky-wide white of it
and she in that green print dress she loved to wear

so vivid I am almost there again,

but it isn't the dress, or her, it's purely
the colour that pulls me back,
the *verde que te quiero verde* in this world that never
ceases, while we go on passing through
as ceaselessly, though always

changing, *verde que te*
quiero—and, just for a moment, I want to stay
her hand and say
we never eat heart any more, or not
in this house; we never eat

liver or tripe, or pigs' trotters simmered for hours
on low heat to draw
the juices—but when I turn to where she was,
my mother is gone and the chair
is empty, like the dead space in a wood

after a tree is felled, or to be more precise,
like the chair in the famous van Gogh, the "empty place"
he painted when Gauguin left, the light from the gas lamp
blue on the polished wood and the stem of a candle,
perfectly clear and almost too vivid to bear

V Coda: Fake Cochineal

We played the game of dying like the fade
of rainfall in a small apartment block
in Cracow
—which I think we must have known
from motion pictures—

not the kind of place
to grow wisteria, though something in the sound
the pigeons made would make us think again
of last year's gold.

And so it darkened. Trampled leaves and snow
like scabs of manna, wasting in a crown
of butcher's broom.

It only took one wolf to make the forest
large again, a splash of sandalwood
to parse a finch, a suitcase on the stairs,

then, later, in the cutting, wakeful dogs
and empty boxcars, bright with frost and lye.

III. 1979 年自畫像

「無論是甚麼痛苦，他不能在一度懷疑，
而且日漸荒唐的世界，重獲心滿意足。」
——辛克萊・劉易斯

彷彿他有一個巴比倫可以失去
彷彿他有多年的母愛被沖刷走

他假裝皮膚是別出心裁的
一種成熟延遲得剛剛好

讓他記住雨水；
雖然不能持續，這段

關於凝結的床單
還有冰毒的敘述

是他在《男孩人生》中所知的一切
不會發出肉凍或公平競賽的惡臭

沒有人在那裏告訴他：心臟
主要是油脂和肌肉，家

比起長居之所更像出租屋，
而夏天來得太早，乾葉

在塵土中變成粉末，污水坑
在後街結成硬塊，被頭髮堵塞。

在城市最遠的邊緣，
動物在血與夜的畜欄裏

被打量，成為漢堡的肉扒
使遊人長胖，肥滿白淨，

花言巧語如情景戲劇中的頂嘴。
破曉時分，唇上有冧酒和香水，

他瞌睡點頭，從睡到醒，又為睡
而睡，直到火車漸漸減速

走在一段火絨色樹叢邊上，光
與霧飛快略過草地和所有

常見的垃圾，玻璃樽碎片，
舊啤酒罐，報紙紙捻，塑料網布。

有一會兒，他在自己的氣息中唱
「總有出路」——關於

骨頭軟腐的記憶。倏然
他想再要同樣事物，同樣的話，同樣的目光，

同一首老歌中同樣的結局完好的故事
「總有出路」，畢竟，

他知道，來世
有這樣的人

精於引導門診病人回到病房
打開檯燈，城市終於退卻了

門鎖中的鑰匙輕輕轉動
他必須相信

當他致欣喜若狂的時候
他會知道自己一向所愛的是甚麼。

IV. 難以忘懷

「我希望德漢看看我的習作，一支點著了的蠟燭和兩本小說（一本黃色，另一本粉紅色）放在空椅上（真的是高更的椅子），一張三十號尺寸的油畫，紅色和綠色的。在今天，我剛才再次繪畫吊燈，我自己的空椅子，有煙管和煙草袋的白色松木椅。在這兩個習作中，一如其他，我嘗試通過純淨的顏色達到光線效果，可能德漢完全明白我想要做到甚麼，如果你將我所寫的相關話題，讀給他聽。」

——梵谷致提奧的信，
1889 年 1 月 17 日

四十年的死者，我的母親在廚房的桌子
將一顆心切成小塊
門口的雨水，很快就會變成雨雪
然後，從這裏到樹林之間
會有雪。

在那個房子，幾分鐘內，
霧氣便會籠罩窗戶
而整個周末，我們本來可以獨處的，
城鎮其餘一切都被遺棄了，據我們所知，
花園以外空無一物，沒有教會，沒有人煙。

如今她在這兒，在我的廚房裏，將一顆心切成小塊：
她的手肘邊放著一小碟鹽，桌子上撒上
一把麵粉，收音機開著，
她如往常般幹活，全神貫注，
廚師刀捕捉冬日中午的光。

我從來不相信有鬼，而我沒有多大願望
要再次看見自己的死者，
但我怎麼能夠不尊重拒絕淡出的事物，
猶如顏料模糊之處，一隻手或一個瓷碗
隱藏著一張再現的原畫，畫中

有一隻拴繩的鳴鳥，還是我們粉刷洗滌室的牆壁時
再一次浮現的深橘色污漬？
感同身受的男孩怎會不大相信
他們告訴我的事情？——

朋友的朋友的朋友
見證了沒有人能解釋的光，
池塘上的一片光亮，幾十年前
沒有人看見，麵包師傅的兒子
沉落冰面，沉落除夕的火水藍之中。

我記得我們有天暫停禮拜日外出散步，
在突如其來的霧中，樹木
在天空廣闊的白色中屏住呼吸
而她穿著她喜歡的綠色印花連衣裙
逼真得我幾乎又相信了，

但是那不是連衣裙，也不是她，純粹只是
色彩把我拉回去，
「綠啊，我多麼愛你這綠色」此世不會
休止，當我們繼續不休止地
度過，雖然總是

在變，「我多麼愛你
這綠色」——然後，短短此刻，我想
阻止她，説
我們再也不吃心了，或者不再
在這間屋子裏吃；我們從來不吃

用文火燉了幾個小時
燉出肉汁的牛肝、牛肚
或豬蹄——但當我轉向她所在之處
我的母親不見了，椅子上
沒有人，好像林地中一棵樹木

倒下以後留下沒有生命的空地，或更準確地説，
好像梵高名畫中的椅子，高更離開時
他畫下的「空間」，煤氣燈的光
拋光木頭上的藍色還有蠟燭幹，
完全清楚，還幾乎逼真得令人難以忍受。

V. 尾聲：假洋紅

我們玩死亡的遊戲
好像在克拉科夫的小公寓樓
逐漸消失的降雨，
——我想我們必須知道
是來自電影——

不是那種長出
紫藤的地方，雖然鴿子的聲息中
有點甚麼讓我們再次想起
去年的金子。

然後它變暗了。被踐踏的葉子和雪
像嗎哪般的結痂，靡廢在花竹柏的花冠上。

只消一隻狼就令森林
再次變大，少許檀香木
拆解雀鳥的語法，樓梯上的行李箱，

那麼，然後，剪報中，狗兒清醒
貨運車箱空虛，霜和石灰，一切都明亮起來。

努諾・朱迪斯（葡萄牙），1949年生於葡萄牙南部阿爾加維，本科畢業於里斯本大學羅曼語言系，1989年獲得文學博士學位。1997年至2004年擔任葡萄牙駐巴黎大使館文化參贊，同時兼任巴黎賈梅士學院主任。他還曾在里斯本新大學教授葡萄牙文學和法國文學。作為葡萄牙當代最有代表性的詩人之一，他著述豐富，涉獵廣泛，除了已發表的大量詩歌外，在散文、戲劇、文學研究與詩歌批評方面也成果豐碩，同時他也為報紙撰稿。他還曾擔任法蘭克福第四十九屆書展葡萄牙文學顧問（該屆葡萄牙為主題國）。2009年，他開始擔任高秉根基金會轄下的文學雜誌 *Colóquio-Letras* 的主編。他多次獲獎，2013年榮獲「伊比利亞—美洲索菲婭皇后詩歌獎」。他的著作已經被翻譯成多種語言，特別是西班牙文、法文、意大利文和阿拉伯文。

Nuno Júdice (Portugal) was born in Algarve, Portugal in 1949. He graduated in Romance Philology from the University of Lisbon and received his doctorate in 1989 with a thesis on Medieval Literature. He served from 1997 to 2004 as the cultural attaché of the Portuguese Embassy in Paris and Director of the Camões Institute also in Paris. He was a teacher of Portuguese and French Literature in the Universidade Nova de Lisboa. He has published studies on theory of literature and Portuguese literature and maintains a regular contributor in the press. He was Commissioner for the area of Portuguese literature representing the 49th Book Fair in Frankfurt, which had Portugal as a country theme. His works are not only about poetry and fiction but also essays, theatre, critical edition and anthology. He is the Director since 2009 of *Colóquio-Letras*, literary magazine of the Calouste Gulbenkian Foundation. In 2013 he received the Poetry Prize Reina Sofia for Ibero-American Poetry. Many of his books are translated in several languages, mainly Spanish, French, Italian and Arabic.

努諾・朱迪斯

NUNO JÚDICE

中文翻譯：姚風

English Translation by Paulo da Costa, Richard Zenith, Ana Hudson and Karen Press

Imagem

O homem que falava sozinho na estação central de munique
que língua falava? Que língua falam os que se perdem assim, nos
corredores das estações de comboio, à noite, quando já nenhum
quiosque vende jornais nem cafés? O homem de
munique não me pediu nada, nem tinha ar de
quem precisasse de alguma coisa, isto é, tinha aquele ar
de quem chegou ao último estado
que é o de quem não precisa nem de si próprio. No entanto,
falou-me: numa língua sem correspondência com linguagem
alguma de entre as possíveis de exprimirem emoção
ou sentimento, limitando-se a uma sequência de sons cuja lógica
a noite contrariava. Perguntar-me-ia se eu compreendia acaso
a sua língua? Ou queria dizer-me o seu nome e de onde vinha
– àquela hora em que não estava nenhum comboio
nem para chegar nem para partir? Se me dissesse isto,
ter-lhe-ia respondido que também eu não esperava ninguém,
nem me despedia de alguém, naquele canto de uma estação
alemã; mas poderia lembrar-lhe que há encontros que só dependem
do acaso, e que não precisam de uma combinação prévia
para se realizarem. – É então que os horóscopos adquirem sentido;
e a própria vida, para além deles, dá um sentido à solidão que empurra
alguém para uma estação deserta, à hora em que já não se compram
jornais nem se tomam cafés, restituindo um resto de alma ao corpo
ausente – o suficiente para que se estabeleça um diálogo, embora
ambos sejamos a sombra do outro. É que, a certas horas da noite,
ninguém pode garantir a sua própria realidade, nem quando outro,
como eu próprio, testemunhou toda a solidão do mundo
arrastada num deambular de frases sem sentido numa estação morta.

影像

那個在慕尼黑中央火車站自言自語的人
說的是甚麼語言？已是夜晚，售賣亭已不賣報紙和咖啡，
而那些在車站長廊遊蕩的人
說的是甚麼語言？慕尼黑的那名男子
沒要我做甚麼，甚至沒要我
做任何表情，也就是說，他到了這種境界，
他誰也不需要，也不需要自己。然而，
他卻和我說話了：一種不等同任何一種
可以表達感情和激情的語言，只是一連串的音節，
其邏輯性與黑夜相悖。我自問，我懂他的語言嗎？
或許他想告訴我他叫甚麼名字？來自何方？
——那個時候已沒有火車了嗎？
出發的？到達的？
如果他告訴我這個，我會回答他說，
我在這個德國車站的一隅，
也無人可等待，也無人可以告別，但我會提醒他，
有些相聚純出於偶然，無需事先安排。
——這樣占星術便獲得了意義；至於生活本身，
除了占星術之外，會賦予孤獨以意義，
而孤獨則把一個人推向已不賣報紙和咖啡的
冷寂車站，把剩餘的靈魂還給不在場的身體
——這足以開始一個對話，雖然我們彼此不過是
對方的影子而已。也就是說，在夜晚的某個時間，
誰也不能保證自己的現實，
甚至當一個像我一樣的他人，
在一個死寂的車站見證了
世界上所有的寂寞如何被拖入
毫無意義的詞語之中的時候。

Image

The man who talked to himself in münich's central station
what language did he speak? What language
speak the ones who are lost like that, in
the platform of train stations, at night, when no
kiosk sells newspapers or coffee? The münich
man asked me for nothing, he didn't even look
as if he needed anything, meaning, he looked
like someone who arrived at the last stage
which is the stage of someone who does not
even need oneself. Although, he spoke to me:
in a tongue not resembling any of the languages
capable of expressing emotion
or feeling, limited to a sequence of sounds whose logic
the night contradicted. Might he be asking me
if by chance I understood his language? Or would he
be wanting to tell me his name and where he was from
at such hour when no train was
about to arrive or leave? If he had told me this,
I would have told him that I also waited for no one,
or that I was not saying goodbye to someone,
in that corner of a german station; although
I could remind him that some meetings only depend
on chance, not requiring a previous arrangement
to take place. – Then horoscopes gain meaning;
and life itself, beyond them, lends a meaning
to the solitude that pushes someone toward an empty station,
at an hour when newspapers are not bought
or coffee drunk, restoring a touch of soul to the absent
body – enough to establish a dialogue, although
we are both each other's shadow. Since, at certain hours
of the night, no one can be certain
of one's reality, not even when another,
like myself, witnessed the entire loneliness of the world
dragged through a meandering of senseless sentences in a dead station.

(Translated by Paulo da Costa)

Receita Para Fazer o Azul

Se quiseres fazer azul,
pega num pedaço de céu e mete-o numa panela grande,
que possas levar ao lume do horizonte;
depois mexe o azul com um resto de vermelho
da madrugada, até que ele se desfaça:
despeja tudo num bacio bem limpo,
para que nada reste das impurezas da tarde.
Por fim, peneira um resto de ouro da areia
do meio dia, até que a cor pegue ao fundo de metal.
Se quiseres, para que as cores se não desprendam
com o tempo, deita no líquido um caroço de pêssego queimado.
Vê-lo-ás desfazer-se, sem deixar sinais de que alguma vez
ali o puseste; e nem o negro da cinza deixará um resto de ocre
na superfície dourada. Podes, então, levantar a cor
até á altura dos olhos, e compara-la com o azul autêntico.
Ambas as cores te parecerão semelhantes, sem que
possas distinguir entre uma e outra.
Assim o fiz – eu, Abraão bem Judá Ibn Haim,
iluminador de Loulé – e deixei a receita a quem quiser,
algum dia, imitar o céu.

藍之配方

如果你想要藍色，
那麼就截取一塊天空，把它放入一個大平底鍋裏，
你可以把鍋放在天際線的篝火上；
然後把天空與晨曦殘留的紅霞一起攪拌，
直至被攪碎：再倒入一個乾淨的盆裏，
為的是不留下下午的雜質。
最後，篩一篩中午的金沙，
直到熬乾水分，顏色濃郁。
如果你希望顏色不因時間而褪色
請把一個燒焦的桃子放進液體。
你要看著它被攪碎，
不能留下你染指的跡象，
也不要讓黑色的灰燼在金色的表面
留下赭色。然後，你可以認真看一看，
並與原色藍進行比較。
你會覺得這兩種藍看起來很相似，
難分彼此。
我就是這樣做的——我，亞伯拉罕·本·猶大·伊本·海姆[1]，
來自羅萊的泥金工匠——我可以把配方給任何
想要仿製藍天的人。

1 譯註：亞伯拉罕·本·猶大·伊本·海姆（Abraão bem Judá Ibn Haim）被視為是用《如何製造顏料》（*O livro de como se fazem as cores*）一書的作者，這是一本十世紀的古書，用居住在葡萄牙的猶太人方言寫成，講述的是如何製作用於泥金裝飾的顏料。詩人寫作動機來自這本書。

Recipe for Making the Colour Blue

If you wish to make the colour blue
take a piece of sky and put it in a pot
large enough to place on the flame of the horizon.
Stir into the blue a pinch of early morning red
until it dissolves. Pour everything
into a brass bowl that has been well washed
to eliminate all the afternoon's impurities.
Finally, sift in a few smidgens of gold from the sand
of midday until the colour adheres to the bottom of the bowl.
To prevent the colours from separating with time,
drop a charred peach pit into the liquid.
It will disintegrate, leaving no telltale
sign, not even – from the black ash – an ochre trace
on the golden surface. You may then raise the colour
to eye level and compare it with genuine blue.
The two colours will look so alike
that you cannot distinguish one from the other.
This was how I did it – I, Abraham ben Judah Ibn Haim,
illuminator from the town of Loulé. And I left the recipe
for whoever, one day, would imitate the sky.

(Translated by Richard Zenith)

Variação Sobre Rosas

Como as rosas selvagens, que nascem
em qualquer canto, o amor também pode nascer
de onde menos esperamos. O seu campo
é infinito: alma e corpo. E, para além deles,
o mundo das sensações, onde se entra sem
bater à porta, como se esta porta estivesse sempre
aberta para quem quiser entrar.

Tu, que me ensinas o que é o
amor, colheste essas rosas selvagens: a sua
púrpura brilha no teu rosto. O seu perfume
corre-te pelo peito, derrama-se no estuário
do ventre, sobe até aos cabelos que se soltam
por entre a brisa dos murmúrios. Roubo aos teus
lábios as suas pétalas.

E se essas rosas não murcham, com
o tempo, é porque o amor as alimenta.

玫瑰變奏曲

就像野玫瑰可以生長
在任何角落，愛情也會在
我們意想不到的地方製造奇跡。
愛情的原野一望無際：身體與靈魂。
此外還有感官世界，
無需敲門即可進入，
好像門扉一直敞開，
人人可入。

是你，教我甚麼是愛，
你採摘了野玫瑰：深紅的花
映照著你的臉龐。芬芳
沿著你的胸脯流溢，在你小腹的河口
恣意汪洋，最後飄升至你在微風絮語中鬆散的秀髮間。
我從你的雙唇間，
竊走玫瑰的花瓣。

如果說這些玫瑰抗拒時間，永不枯萎，
只因愛把它們滋養。

Variation on Roses

Like the wild roses that grow in
any corner, love can also come
from where we least expect it. Its field
is infinite: body and soul. And, beyond them,
the world of sensations, that we enter without
knocking, as if the door was always
open for whoever wishes to go in.

You, who teach me what love is,
have gathered those wild roses: their crimson
colour shines on your face. Their scent
flows down your chest, floods the estuary
of your womb, climbs up to your hair loose
in a breeze of murmurs. From your lips,
I steal their petals.

And if those roses do not fade, with
time, it is because they're nourished by love.

(Translated by Ana Hudson)

Branco

Não queiras saber o que é o branco para
além do branco, a ilusão de que o mar
se prolonga nesse mar que o branco
devora, com os lábios do vento; nem
interrogues o rosto que se esconde
no horizonte do branco, onde só o
silêncio te dá a resposta que ignoras.

No entanto, se o olhar que esse
horizonte te devolve tem a luz do
rosto que só no branco entrevês,
quando o vento empurra as cortinas
do mar, talvez reconheças no seu
fundo o corpo que habita o céu
em que o branco coincide com o mar.

E nos olhos fechados de um rosto
preso à cama da madrugada, o branco
do horizonte submerge o mar que
avança por dentro do branco, como se
a luz do dia que o vento te abre
não fosse branca, como esse branco
lençol que esconde o corpo sob o mar.

E em cada nuvem que passa no branco
do céu, um rosto revela o branco
para além do horizonte que o branco descobre.

白

你一定不想知道白色之外的白色
是甚麼，是幻覺：大海在大海中延伸，
白色用風的嘴唇將其吞噬，
你也不要詢問
被白色的天際線隱匿的面孔，
只有寂靜才會告訴你
你不知道的答案。

然而，當風撩動起大海的面紗，
如果天際線還給你目光
你可以瞥見陽光的面孔，
你在白色中才能辨認的面孔，
也許你將在大海的深處認出身體
它棲居於天空，白色與大海融為一體。

在一張依偎著黎明睡床的臉上，
在閉上眼睛中，白色的
天際線潛入大海
潛入白的深處，就像風為你打開
白晝之光不是白色的，
就像白色的圍巾
在大海下隱藏的身體。

而在每一朵掠過天空之白的雲
都有一張臉，顯示著白色
在天際線以外發現的白色。

Whiteness

Don't interrogate whiteness
beyond whiteness, the illusion of a sea
begun again in the one that the
whiteness devours, with its lips of wind;
nor the face of whiteness hidden
on the horizon, where only silence
answers your lack of consciousness.

Yet, if the gaze that
this horizon returns to you has the brightness of a
face only glimpsed in the whiteness
when the wind lifts the veils
of the sea, then perhaps you will make out
in its depths the body whose dwelling is
this sky where whiteness and the sea coincide.

And in the closed eyes of a face
held back by the bed of dawn, the whiteness
of the horizon submerges the sea that
retreats inside whiteness, as if the
light of day that the wind opens
to you were not white, white as
these sheets that hide the body beneath the sea.

And in each cloud that passes in the whiteness
of the sky, a face reveals the whiteness
beyond the horizon that whiteness uncovers.

(Translated by Karen Press)

林舜玲（香港），曾負笈新加坡及美國留學。她前任香港大學教授，2012年退休，並曾為傅爾布萊特基金、英國文化協會及數家大學的訪問學人。代表著作包括 *Woman to Woman and Other Poems*（1997）、*Water Wood Pure Splendour*（2001）和 *A Pond in the Sky*（2013），部分詩作並獲譯成德文、意大利文及其他語言。林舜玲於2008年獲愛荷華大學頒授寫作榮譽院士，並於意大利諾西德國際詩歌比賽奪得「特別表揚獎」。2009年，她榮獲香港民政事務局「嘉許狀」，以誌她於國際藝文活動的建樹。林舜玲致力學術研究，其著作 *Language Education in China: Policy and Experience from 1949*（香港大學出版社，2005），論證新穎，領先同儕。近年她鑽研亞洲的英語詩作，備受矚目，其論著 *Becoming Poets: The Asian English Experience*（Peter Lang, 2014）「參照之廣、探究之深」，實為「亞洲英語體驗的有力考察」（*Asiatic*，2015年12月號，書評人：Murari Prasad）。

Agnes S. L. Lam (Hong Kong) studied in Singapore and America. In 2012, she retired as Professor from the University of Hong Kong. She also held visitorships from Fulbright, the British Council and several universities at different times. Representative works include: *Woman to Woman and Other Poems* (1997), *Water Wood Pure Splendour* (2001) and *A Pond in the Sky* (2013). Some of her poems have been translated into German, Italian and other languages. An Honorary Fellow in Writing by the University of Iowa (2008), she was awarded the Nosside International Poetry Prize (Special Mention, 2008). In 2009, she also received a Commendation from the Home Affairs Bureau, HKSAR, in recognition of her outstanding achievements in international arts and cultural activities. As a researcher, she has long been well known for her pioneering volume, *Language Education in China: Policy and Experience from 1949* (HKU Press, 2005). More recently, she is also noted for her work on Asian poetry in English. Her book, *Becoming Poets: The Asian English Experience* (Peter Lang, 2014), "with its breadth of reference and depth of investigation," has been hailed as "a cogent assessment of the Asian English experience" (*Asiatic*, December 2015, reviewer: Murari Prasad).

林舜玲

AGNES S. L. LAM

中文翻譯：陳嘉恩

White Orchids on Concrete

Waking on my third morning
in Balay Internasyonal, I found
white orchids on the concrete wall,

six or seven of them growing
without stems or leaves or roots,
arched above the foot of my bed.

"What do they mean?" I wondered
throughout my Saturday outing
in Ayala with my Filipino friend,

sauntering through the Greenbelts
of yuppie pubs, designers' republic,
bamboo gardens with carp in the ponds…

At the museum, we walked through millennia
of Filipino history – the Chinese, the Muslims,
the Spanish, the Americans, the Japanese,

and finally the Filipinos – the same old story
played out almost to a cue on different soils
in Asia. What happened five centuries ago,

even one century before, could be forgiven,
if not forgotten. But twenty-odd years ago,
my Filipino sister was not yet thirty when

she joined millions on the streets soon after
I saw on television in America the murder of
Ninoy Aquino stepping off the plane in Manila.

As we stood among the sea of faces on film
in the museum, tears came. And I understood
what the white orchids on concrete meant.

22 February 2010, the anniversary of the People Power Revolution,
University of the Philippines Balay Internasyonal, for Lily Rose

混凝土上的白蘭花

第三天早上醒來
於國際賓館，我看見
混凝土牆上的白蘭花

長有六七株
沒有莖或葉或根，
拱立在我的床腳之上。

「它們是甚麼意思？」我想知道，
星期六郊遊時一直想。
在愛雅拉，我跟隨菲律賓朋友

漫步綠化帶
串連優皮酒吧、設計師共和國
竹子園裏的池塘有鯉魚……

博物館內，我們穿越了一千年的
菲律賓歷史——華人、穆斯林、
西班牙人、美國人、日本人，

還有菲律賓人——一樣的老故事，
不同的土壤上，仿如按照提示演出
於亞洲。五個世紀前發生過的事情，

甚至一世紀前發生過的，都可以被原諒，
如果沒有被人遺忘。可是二十多年前，
我的菲律賓姐妹還不到三十歲，當時

她隨百萬民眾上街，不久之前，
我在美國電視看見尼諾．阿基諾
在馬尼拉甫下機，即遭殺害。

影片中人臉如海，我們站在中間
在博物館裏，流下淚來。我明白了
混凝土上的白蘭花是甚麼意思。

2010年2月22日，人民力量革命週年紀念，
菲律賓大學國際賓館，獻給Lily Rose

Time to Go

1967 –
we stayed put at home as
there were bombs in the streets.

1989 –
the smell of blood afar,
we all marched down Queensway.

2014 –
for a month and more days,
you have camped on the roads.

You have spoken your mind.
We have heard every word.
Even those who didn't care
now watch the news daily.

So try to listen please
to voices not your own.
To prison or to death
is not the only way.

Move to Tamar Park if
you still want to protest.
Or form your own party
to get into LegCo.

It's not the traffic jams.
It's not the business lost.
We just want to leave you
a place you can call home.

Time to go home, my friends.
It is still not too late.
No one would laugh at you.
We were all there before.

One fine day some winter,
you will walk down the streets,
feel the sun on your face.

In your mind, you may still
see the tents and your friends,
the mobile lights at night…

but you may wonder where
did all the hatred go,
what dreams were really dreamt…

31 October 2014, the 34th day of Occupy Central, Admiralty

是時候走了

1967年——
我們安守家中，
因為街上有炸彈。

1989年——
遠方飄來血腥，
我們所有人遊行到金鐘道。

2014年——
一個月再多數天，
你在馬路上紮營。

你說出了你的心聲，
我們每個字都聽見了。
再漠不關心的人，
現在每天都看新聞。

所以，請細心聆聽
不屬於你自己的聲音。
監獄或者死亡
不是唯一的出路。

移師添馬艦去，假如
你還想抗議，
或組成你自己的政黨，
進軍立法會。

堵車不要緊，
丟了生意不要緊，
我們只想留給你
一個你可以喊一聲「家」的地方。

是時候回家了，我的朋友，
現在還不算太遲。
沒有人會取笑你，
我們都在那裏待過。

在晴朗的一天，某個冬天，
你會走在街上，
感到太陽曬在臉上。

你在心中，可能依然
看見帳篷和你的友伴，
夜裏手機的燈光……

可是你或會感到疑惑，
仇恨到哪裏去了，
夢裏到底夢見甚麼……

2014年10月31日，「佔領中環」第34天，金鐘

Poppies by the Motorway

You cannot touch them.
You cannot take clear photos of them.
They seem to grow only by the motorway in the wild.

Remembering the dead.
Remembering the war, the turmoil after.
Not to be found in the city centres where tourists lunch on sidewalks.

The same red as the coat my Polish friend left.
On a stone bench under a tree by the Zakopane post office in the
mountains.
No one would take it.

The rain soaks it wet.
The sun dries it, time after time, season after season.
No one would take it, thinking the owner would come back.

Waiting to belong...

4 June 2014, on the road to Torun, for Beata

公路旁的紅罌粟

你不可以觸摸它們，
你不可以替它們拍清楚的照片，
它們似乎只會野生在公路旁。

惦記著死者，
惦記著戰爭、之後的動亂。
遊客在行人道上午餐的市中心，不會找到

同一抹紅色，好比我的波蘭朋友留下的外套，
在山中扎科柏內郵局旁樹下的石長凳上，
沒有人會拿走。

雨水弄濕它，
太陽曬乾它，一次又一次，一季復一季，
沒有人會拿走，想著物主將會回來。

等待屬於……

2014年6月4日，往托倫的路上，獻給Beata

瑟梅茲定・梅赫梅迪維奇（波斯尼亞），1960年出生於圖茲拉，波斯尼亞，曾就讀於薩拉熱窩大學。1994年，他與其他五位波斯尼亞作家一同獲得國際作家筆會（PEN）頒發的赫爾曼・哈默特獎，以表彰他們在戰火之中堅守民主信念。梅赫梅迪維奇於1996年以政治難民身份到達美國。他出版的著作包括《薩拉熱窩藍調》(1992)、《亞歷山大城九座》(2002)、《蘇維埃電腦》(2011)、《和一個信差包的自畫像》(2012)、《穆罕默德、紅色香蕉和雪花》(2017)。他目前住在美國維吉尼亞州的阿靈頓。

Semezdin Mehmedinović (Bosnia) was born in Tuzla, Bosnia in 1960, and was educated at the University of Sarajevo. In 1994, with five other Bosnian writers, he received the Hellman-Hammet Award from PEN for persistence in preserving democracy in the midst of war. Mehmedinović arrived in the United States as a political refugee in 1996. His books include *Sarajevo Blues* (1992), *Nine Alexandrias* (2002), *Soviet Computer* (2011), *Self-portrait With a Messenger Bag* (2012) and *Me'med, Red Banana and Snowflake* (2017). He currently lives in Arlington, Virginia, USA.

瑟梅茲定・梅赫梅迪維奇

SEMEZDIN MEHMEDINOVIĆ

中文翻譯：黃峪、Marija Todorova
English translation by Ammiel Alcalay

Devet Alexandrija

Prema mome proračunu, koji mogućno nije potpun,
U Americi je devet gradova s imenom Alexandria.
Kartografija novog
Nastala je na principu ucrtavanja
Starog svijeta preko oceanskog indiga...

Jedino tako je zamisliv
Moj put preko kontinenta:
U prelasku iz jedne Alexandrije u drugu
Neprestano stižući u isti grad.

I samo uz potpuno uvjerenje
Da je cjelina svijeta sačuvana
Mogu zamisliti pokret
Iz jedne u drugu američku Alexandriju,
Na isti egipatski dok

亞歷山大城九座

也許並不全面，但我猜想
美國至少有九個城市叫做亞歷山大
新世界的地圖必須根據
測量舊世界的方法
複寫在靛藍的海洋上……

只有一個方法能讓我
穿州過市去旅行：
從一個亞歷山大城到另一個
總是抵達同一個城市

我只能肯定一件事
這個世界仍然保持完整
我能否想像自己從一個
美國的亞歷山大城到另一個
在同一個埃及的港口

NINE ALEXANDRAS

Maybe that isn't all of them but the way I figure it
There are at least nine cities in America called Alexandria.
Cartography of the new had to be based on the
Principle of tracing the old world
Through an ocean of indigo...

The only thing that makes
My trip across country imaginable is this:
Going from one Alexandria to another
I can't help but get to the same city.

And only by knowing for sure
That the world is still in one piece
Can I imagine moving from one
American Alexandria to another,
On the same Egyptian dock

Istok i Zapad

Zanimljivo je kako prve riječi, povremeno
Obnavljaju puni krug značenja
Kao što se unutrašnjost vagona
Ispunja putnicima pred polazak voza:

U ovom trenu, recimo, *istok* i *zapad*,
Izmišljeni da tijelo u pustoši kontinenta
Odredi svoje mjesto u odnosu na zvijezde,
Znače više od mape
Na čijoj istočnoj je Mecca
A na zapadnoj strani Los Angeles.

To su probuđene strane svijeta
Iako sve izgleda krajnje bezazleno:
Ja putujem na zapad, a u beskonačnom nizu
Ajfelovi strujni tornjevi na istok, prema Parizu

東與西

有趣的是，頭幾個詞語，有時候
會把整個意義圓圈都重置
就像火車出發之前
車廂裏就裝滿了乘客

在這一刻，比如說，*東方*與*西方*
被發明，好讓大陸的荒原之上，這具身軀
可以根據遙遠群星來自行定位
比起東面有麥加
而西面有洛杉磯的地圖
這發明更有意義

他們是世界已覺醒的那一邊
即使所有的事情都看起來全然無害：
我向西方旅行，而一行無盡的電線塔
一路向東，如同埃菲爾鐵塔，面朝巴黎

EAST AND WEST

Interesting how primary words
Square the circle of meaning every now and then
The way the inside of a wagon
Fills with passengers right before a train departs:

Right now, for instance, *east* and *west*,
Invented so a body could orient itself
By the stars in the desolate expanse,
Mean more than maps
Where Mecca's on the east side and
Los Angeles on the west.

These are the waking ends of the world
And it all seems so innocent:
I'm going west but there's an endless series of
Towers to the east, electric grid like Eiffel's, facing Paris

Funkcija srca

Nasmijani kardiolog s New Zealanda
Na američkoj turneji tumači otkriće
Da ljudsko srce proizvodi vrstu hormona
O kojem do sada ništa nismo znali.

Dok objašnjava posljedice svoga otkrića,
On uzvraća pozdrav radnicima uz prugu
Koji ispod žutih šljemova mašu vozu
I jednoj ženi, također, što s verande maše vozu.

Tek u njegovom društvu obraćam pažnju
Na, valjda, jedini ritual pruge:
Ljudi što ostaju, mašu vozu.
Nasmijani kardiolog zna da je pozdrav upućen njemu
I da je tolika usamljenost kontinenta
Nastala iz zapuštene funkcije srca

心之功能

一個微笑的新西蘭心臟科專家
來美國旅行，途中描述他的發現：
人類心臟會生成一種荷爾蒙
至今還成分未明

在描述自己研究的影響時
他回應著鐵路員工的問好
他們戴著黃色安全帽向著火車揮手
他也回應著一位女子，她從陽台向火車揮手

只有和他一起時，我才留意到
這或許是鐵路的唯一儀式：
人們駐足，對火車揮手
笑容滿面的心臟專家知道他們向他問好
也知道這片大陸上所有的寂寞
都來自於被遺忘的心之功能

FUNCTIONS OF THE HEART

On his American tour the smiling
Cardiologist from New Zealand explains his discovery
About the human heart producing a type of hormone
We knew nothing about till now

As he explains the consequences of this discovery
He returns the greetings of the workers on the track
Waving at the train from under their yellow helmets
And a woman, too, waving from her deck.

It's only in his company that I notice this
Peculiar, almost uniquely railway ritual:
The people who stay, wave at the trains.
The smiling cardiologist knows the greetings are
Meant for him and that such continental isolation
Must have originated in functions the heart abandoned

Mit i tekst

U ovom trenu, vidim stvarnog kauboja,
I to je prvi put da ga gledam direktnim sjajem.
Istog sam, toliko puta,
Vidio na reklamnim fotografijama za marlboro:

U ime mojih očiju, neko je ranije istražio
Taj mit, valjda, ravnopravan *Grčkim mitovima*
Dvotomne hrestomatije Roberta Gravesa.

I cijeli kontinent je već neko za mene otkrio,
Što znači: ničega više nepoznatog.
Kažu da je, okružen knjigama,
Na pitanje: «Da li ste ikad bili u Grčkoj?»
Heidegger odgovorio: «Nisam.»
I nakon kratke pauze, ponovio: «Nisam.
Ali je moj sin bio tamo»

神話與文本

在此刻，我看到一個真正的牛仔
這是我第一次好好打量
容光煥發的他
當然，我也在萬寶路香煙廣告的照片上
見過他很多次：

幸好，有人已經研究過
這個神話，我猜想，與羅伯特・格雷夫編輯的
兩卷本《希臘神話》相同

而有人已經為我發現了整片大陸
也就是說：再也沒有未知之地
據說，在書本圍繞之中
當被人問到：「你去過希臘嗎？」
海德格爾回答：「沒有。」
在簡短停頓之後，他說：「沒有，
但我的兒子去過。」

MYTH AND TEXT

Right now I see a real cowboy
And it's the first time I've been able to stare right at one.
In all his glory.
Of course, I've seen his like on Marlboro ads many a time:

Just for my sake, someone once looked into it,
A myth that might be equal to *Greek Myths*,
the two volume compendium by Robert Graves.

It was like the entire continent had already
Been discovered for me, and there was nothing left for me to find out.
They say that, surrounded by books,
To the question "Have you ever been to Greece"
Heidegger answered: "I haven't."
And after a brief pause, he repeated: "I haven't.
But my son has."

Zastava

Napredujući kroz Mojave Desert,
Valjda pod dojmom dnevne stvarnosti,
Usnio leptira s dizajnom američke zastave
Integriranim u krila prozirna kao flis-papir.

Duž cijelog kontinenta, inače,
Gledao sam zastave, zavodljiv odnos
Boja koje sam zavolio
Nakon prve scene iz filma *Paris, Texas*.

Ali u povodu zastave, ljudske namjere
Uzimam s krajnjim nepovjerenjem
I kao falsifikat u odnosu na čistu formu
Iz sna: pretvorena u zračni objekt
I u stvarnosti kontinenta: zastava
Postoji kao čista namjera vjetra

一面旗幟

旅途經過莫哈維沙漠
也許受到遠古現實的影響
我夢見了一隻蝴蝶雙翅上印著美國國旗
半透明如同防油紙

穿越整個大陸的時候
我一路上都看見這些旗幟，它那極具誘惑力的
顏色混搭，在我看完《巴黎，德州》電影
第一幕之後便已愛上

但我並不相信人類的
意圖以及那些旗幟升起的場合
他們徹底虛假，不像我夢想
的純粹形式：形狀變成一個空中漂浮的物體
而這片大陸的現實——一面旗幟只會
在風的純粹意圖中存在

FLAG

Pushing ahead through the Mojave desert,
Maybe under the influence of events in the news,
I dreamt about a butterfly with an American flag
Etched into its wings, delicate as wrapping tissue.

I saw flags anyways, the whole length of the
Continent, an enticing array of
Colors I'd already fallen in love with
After the first scene in *Paris, Texas*.

But I put no faith at all in people's
Intentions and the occasions flags give rise to,
They're just plain fake, not like the pure forms
Of my dream: morphed into an airborne object
And the land's actuality—a flag exists only
As the wind's unadulterated intention

喬治．澤提斯（英國），1948 年生於匈牙利布達佩斯，1956 年匈牙利革命時隨家人移居英格蘭，在倫敦長大，曾在利茲和倫敦兩座城市學習過油畫。著有十五本詩集，譯有十數本匈牙利文學作品。第一本詩集 *The Slant Door*（1979）獲 Faber 紀念獎。2014 年憑詩集 *Reel* 獲 T. S. Eliot 詩歌獎，此前 *The Burning of Books* 和 *Bad Machine* 兩次入選該獎項的最終候選名單。兒童詩集 *In the Land of the Giants* 獲 CLPE 最佳兒童詩歌獎。澤提斯翻譯的匈牙利文學贏得多項國際文學獎，其中克拉斯納霍凱的《撒旦探戈》的英譯本贏得2013 年美國最佳翻譯書獎及2014 年布克國際文學獎。現為英國皇家文學協會成員、匈牙利 Széchenу 文學院院士。最近發表的詩集為 *Mapping the Delta*（2016）。

George Szirtes (United Kingdom) was born in Budapest in 1948 and came to England as a refugee with his parents and younger brother following the Hungarian Uprising of 1956. He grew up in London and trained as a painter in Leeds and London. He is the author of some fifteen books of poetry, roughly the same of translation from Hungarian. His first, *The Slant Door* (1979) was joint winner of the Faber Memorial Prize. In 2004 he won the T. S. Eliot Prize for *Reel*, and was shortlisted for the prize again in 2009 for *The Burning of the Books* and for *Bad Machine* (2013). His translations from Hungarian have won various international prizes such as the Best Translated Book Award in the USA for László Krasznahorkai's *Satantango* (2013) which also received the translator's prize in the Man Booker International 2014, and his latest book for children, *In the Land of the Giants* won the CLPE Prize for best collection of poetry for children, also in 2013. He is a Fellow of the Royal Society of Literature in the UK and of the Széchenу Academy of Arts and Letters in Hungary. His latest book of poems is *Mapping the Delta* (2016).

喬治・澤提斯

GEORGE SZIRTES

中文翻譯：宋子江

Like a Black Bird

Like a black bird against snow, he flapped
Over the path, his overcoat billowing
In the cold wind as if he had trapped

The whole sky in it. We watched trees swing
Behind him, lurching drunkenly, blurred
Bare twigs and branches, scrawny bits of string,

And as we gazed ahead the snowflakes purred
In our ears, whispering the afternoon
Which grew steadily darker and more furred.

His face was in shadow, but we'd see it soon.
As he approached it slowly gathered shape:
His nose, in profile, was a broken moon,

His hat a soft black hill bound round with tape,
His raised lapels held his enormous eyes
Between them. The winter seemed to drape

Itself about him as if to apologise
For its own fierceness, hoping to grow warm
Through physical contact, and we, likewise,

Ran towards him, against a grainy storm
Of light and damp. It was so long ago
And life was then in quite another form,

When there were blacker days and thicker snow.

from Reel *(2004)*

猶如一隻黑鳥

猶如一隻黑鳥於雪上，拍翅
穿過小徑，他的大衣在冷風中
翻滾，彷彿他把整個天空

都捕在懷裏。我們看樹木
在他身後晃動，朦朧禿枝
如線頭瘦削，踉蹌醉步

我們向前凝望，雪片咕噥
耳邊，細訴這個下午
逐漸暗淡，逐漸蓬絨

他的臉仍在陰影裏，但很快就能看見
他慢慢接近，漸漸拾掇形態
鼻子的剪影輪廓是一輪裂開的月亮

他的帽子是鬆垮的黑色丘陵，捆綁著膠帶
他的翻領返起，托著巨大的眼睛
冬天似乎展開四肢躺在

他身邊，彷彿在為自己的冷冽
致歉，希望通過身體接觸
暖和起來，而我們，也一樣

向他跑過去，頂著光芒
和濡濕的風暴。那已是往事了
生活完全是另一副模樣

日子更黑，雪也更厚

選自 Reel *(2004)*

No Sooner Can a Child

No sooner can a child walk and make out his letters
Than he is surrendered to the hard pavement
Of any ill-built street where others are skipping
In squares among grids that are numbered
Or leaping through ropes, screaming incoherencies,
Under systems of stars that are inexplicable,
Past policemen with batons and revolvers in their holsters,
In the stern light of midday between short hard-edged shadows
That cut them in two so that half is invisible
Or else dazzled and no one can make out the letters
Of street signs, of names on shop windows, of notices in the park
Or even begin to discriminate between delicate shades
Of small print in the sheet of newspaper blown along the gutter.
No sooner can a child walk than he has to start running
And bones that are brittle get broken so that he must read
The harsh rules of the body, its blood, flesh and skin,
The codes inscribed in the nerve-cells he has inherited
From nameless uncles, from fly-by-night affairs
That establish the book of his being, the fool's idiolect
He must speak all his life. Ideas are eternal
And even the match I hold to this page is impotent
Because this very moment someone is remembering
The syntax and rhythm of phrases that have detached themselves
From flammable editions, and the grammar keeps reforming
Hurtling down the street where the child plays
And stumbles, blowing in his face like a paper bag
Adhering to his features, so when he peels it away
The face remains there, its features encrypted
Then flies past him into libraries, into volumes of speech
No one can hear or pronounce.

from The Burning of the Books *(2009)*

孩子剛一開始……

孩子剛一開始走路和認字
就在劣建的街道上敗倒於
堅硬的地面。他人都跨過
方格陣中帶有號碼的方磚
或跳過繩子，大呼小叫，步調紊亂
在無法解釋的宇宙繁星系統之下。
過去的警察，警棍和手槍在皮套裏
正午嚴峻的日光裏，短小鮮明的影子
把它們切成兩半，所以不是看不見
就是太刺眼。沒有人看得清街道上的字
街道名、店鋪櫥窗上的牌子、公園告示
甚至根本看不出沿著水溝翻飛的報紙上
細小字粒之間精緻的陰影
孩子剛一開始走路就不得不跑起來
就會摔斷脆弱的骨頭，所以他必須讀懂
嚴苛的身體規律，它的血、肉和皮膚
鐫刻在神經細胞上的法典，遺傳自
無名無姓的大叔，夜逃的偷情
締造他的存在之書，傻瓜的用語
他必須言說一生。意念是永恆的
即使我把火柴拿到紙上也無能為力
因為就在此刻，有人正在記起
片語的句法和節奏從可燃的版本中
脫離，語法不斷改良
飛快衝落孩子玩耍
和摔倒的街道上，吹到他的臉上
像一個紙袋蓋著容貌。把它剝下來
臉依舊存在，容貌加密
穿過他飛進圖書館化作卷卷言語
無人聽見，無人宣講

選自 The Burning of the Books *(2009)*

Some Sayings About the Snake

After Helen Rousseau

The snake is imaginary, even in life.

We know it from a ribbon by its windings.

We know it by its movement, eyes, and fangs.

We know it from the apprehension we feel dreaming of it.

The snake arrives at dawn with the first light.

It enters through the ear and exits through the navel.

It coils itself within the gut and heart.

The snake is the primal scream in the grass.

It coils around the limbs of man and tree.

It lives under a stone in the guilty conscience.

It is necklace and armlet and bangle and song.

The snake is the air in a hollow tube.

The snake measures time the way man measures cloth.

The snake spells out its name in the sand.

The snake lives at the edges of life.

When the snake enters a book, the book closes.

from Bad Machine *(2013)*

關於蛇的諺語

（讀Helen Rousseau）

蛇是想像而已，在生活中亦然。

我們從絲帶的蜷曲中認識蛇。

我們從動靜、眼睛和獠牙中認識蛇。

我們從夢見牠時感覺到的焦慮中認識蛇。

蛇在清晨的第一絲曙光中到來。

蛇鑽進耳朵，鑽出肚臍。

蛇踡縮在內臟的心臟裏面。

蛇是草叢裏原初的吶喊。

蛇纏繞人的四肢、樹的枝節。

蛇活在良心有愧的石頭底下。

蛇是項鏈、是臂環、是手鐲、是歌。

蛇是空洞試管中的空氣。

蛇量度時間正如人量度布料。

蛇在砂裏面說出自己的名字。

蛇活在生活的邊緣。

蛇一旦進入書中，書就會合上。

選自 Bad Machine *(2013)*

Minimenta: Postcards to Anselm Kiefer

(Excerpt)

2. Wind, Cloud, Drilling

How often have we watched trees
move against dark cloud, their frail
armature part collapsed, part thrust
against the wind, the leaf-sail
of each bud billowing to squeeze
light from dark, energy from dust?

*

Unrest. The un-ness of things. Twig
like a broken No. Concrete steps.
A drill. A bulldozer. The cold lips
of November pursed for a kiss
that is more like a blow and all this
far too late, too troubled and too big.

*

Everywhere the human voice. How can
we help but hear it in grass and air?
Even a wall is only a tall noise with brick
syntax. High clouds whisper human
non-sequiturs that turn to rain. Where
can we hide? Why this sense of panic?

*

A man and woman in a field. The rain
starts and they take shelter. The grass
runs all one way. They embrace. They hold
each other as if they could not do so ever again.
Above them leaves fold and unfold
in the downpour that will quickly pass.

*

The construction site constructing.
The square empty but for machinery.
The cafeteria with its litter of trays.

Everywhere institutions. The lost days.
All this will be broken up, everything.
There will be no drama, only scenery.

*

And then he turned to her and ran
the back of his hand against her cheek
very lightly. It was as if wind had stroked any
surface whatsoever. He was an old man
or a young man, and she could not speak
or find words because there were too many.

from Bad Machine *(2013)*

Minimenta：給Anselm Kiefer的明信片

（節錄）

2. 風、雲、鑽研

我們有多經常看見樹木
移向烏雲？它們的脆弱
甲胄，部分凹陷，部分
凸向風中，每一朵花蕾的
葉帆都在翻滾，從黑暗裏
擠出光芒，從塵埃中擠出力量。

*

不安。事物「不」的性質。嫩枝
猶如一個破碎的「不」。實在的腳步。
一把電鑽。一架推土機。十一月
冰冷的嘴唇嘟起，只為一個吻
卻更像一下擊打，而這一切
都太遲、太煩、太大了。

*

每個地方都有人聲。我們又
怎能不在草叢和空氣中聽見？
一扇牆也只是一聲由磚頭語法
砌高的噪音。高處的雲輕訴
人之「*不續*」而化作雨水。我們
能躲在哪裏？為何感到恐慌？

*

男人和女人在一片田野上。雨
下了，他們躲避。草
沿著同一個方向奔跑。他們擁抱
彷彿可一不可再。
他們頭上的葉叢捲縮又舒展
暴雨很快就下完了。

*

建築工地在建築。
廣場空曠只為機械。
快餐店裏亂丟著餐盤。

機構無處不在。失去的日子。
這一切都會破碎，這一切。
沒有戲劇性，只有情景。

*

然而他轉身面向她
手背掃過她的臉頰
非常輕，猶如柔風撫摸
事物的表面。他是個老人
還是個年輕人，而她不能說話
還是話太多不知如何說起？

選自 Bad Machine *(2013)*

馬克・卓狄尼（澳洲），當代澳洲著名詩人、散文家，在澳洲各地學校教寫作，參加過澳洲、美國和英國等地的文學節。曾獲Montreal 詩歌獎、Cardiff 詩歌獎、Blake 詩歌獎、Newcastle 詩歌獎、Calibre 散文獎。兩次獲頒澳洲國內的州長文學獎。他所著的風景回憶錄 *The Blue Plateau* 入選澳洲總理文學獎。2016 年獲ACU 詩歌獎；2017 年獲Ron Pretty 詩歌獎。

Mark Tredinnick (Australia) is a celebrated poet, essayist, and writing teacher. His honours include the Montreal and Cardiff Poetry Prizes, The Blake and Newcastle Poetry Prizes, two Premiers' Literature Awards, and the Calibre Essay Prize. *The Blue Plateau*, his landscape memoir, shortlisted for the Prime Minister's Prize. He travels and teaches widely, in schools and at festivals, through Australia and in the US and UK. In 2016 his poem "The Horse" won the ACU Poetry Prize; in March 2017, his poem "Panic Very Softly, Love" won the Ron Pretty Poetry Prize.

馬克・卓狄尼

MARK TREDINNICK

中文翻譯：宋子江、鄭政恆

Egret in a Ploughed Field

At the close of day I watch an egret
nail a soft landing in a ploughed field and earth
The shallow sky. The ground is scoured where she falls, a soul
Turned, like a pocket, inside out, and the bird wanders
the black rows, scoring them loosely with its one bright note.

She makes an inverse music, it seems to me,
plucking the furrows
For what they may yield, an improvised notation
That erases itself writing itself down, singing the earth back silently
into the belly of a bird, a reverie

In negative, which wakes the dawning dark
all the way back to its beginning again. The bird's random waltz
Down unwalled streets goes on—this little
Night music, these white field notes that pull up day's ends by the roots
and leaf out the night—

Until the darker music, furloughed
here by day, swells and the bird fades, swallowed
By what she'd divined. And she leaves the darkness more luminously dark
Around the hole she cuts in it, flying blind
the ploughed field home to roost.

犁田白鷺

白天將盡，我看著一隻白鷺
輕輕降落，釘在犁田泥土上
天空淺淺的。她降落的地面都抹刷乾淨了，一具靈魂
反轉，猶如一個口袋，裏朝外。白鷺遊蕩在
黑色田畦上，用疏落亮白的音符來譜曲

在我看來，她在創造背反的音樂
鉤拔著犁溝
為了它們的產出。這種即興的記譜法
抹去自己書寫的自己，歌唱著大地，默默地把它
唱回白鷺的腹腔裏，一次夢幻

在負片裏喚醒破曉時分的黑暗
又把它送回原初。白鷺隨意跳著華爾茲
跳進沒有圍牆的街道上——一段短短的
夜曲，一串白色的音符，把白天的盡頭連根拔起
讓葉子開出黑夜——

直到更暗的音樂，讓白天暫時解僱
到這裏，直到它膨脹。鳥兒褪色
吞沒在神聖化之中。她把黑暗留在切離的洞口
留下更有亮澤的黑暗，盲盲飛過
犁田家巢。

（宋子江 譯）

The Kingfisher

For Maureen Harris

And so each bird throws the idea of herself
                    ahead of herself, up the river—
A line of spiritual thought without a sinker—
And flies after it. As if the actual could ever hope to reel the ideal in. But so
    it is
That awareness of the Azure Kingfisher—a dark electricity, a plump
Trim elegance of intent—reaches you on the riverbank
                    that last warm Sunday of autumn, split seconds
Before the bird; so that when she passes you at light speed, her name
          is already a bright blue phrase on your tongue, is already
                    the unresolved cadence of your second self.

藍翠鳥

給毛林・哈里斯

每一隻鳥兒都把自我的意念
                    投向自我的前方，河上——
一列心靈思緒，無一下沉——
飛蟲尾隨。彷彿真實有望捲收空想。而這就是
那隻藍翠鳥的意識——一道黑電，一次飛墮
意向有種修束的優雅——觸及河岸上的你
                    秋天最後一個暖和的週日，倏瞬
於鳥兒跟前；當她以光速飛過你跟前，她的名字
          早已是舌頭上亮藍色的片語，早已是
               第二個自我懸而未決的頓挫。

（宋子江 譯）

Lotus Pond

For Sarah

If you want heaven, start in mud.
Begin transfiguration
Where you're stuck. Take your pilgrimage standing
Up to your ankles in sludge. And if the ground binds
and if your boots stick, and if you step
Out of them when you set off; if the odour
On a summer's day, when the water ebbs, is noisome
where you begin, so much more pure

Your thoughts will be when they flower,
so much sweeter the garden's scent when
You breathe it in, so much more like birdsong
Your voice when you begin at last to speak. Start underwater
if you want the sky. Start in the abject
Underworld, if you want the lighted Earth; start among
The throng of ears that cannot hear. Sink in detritus, seed in
the strife that your life, and every life,

Falls into now and then: Serenity
springs from squalor; love is only love if it
Can bear the badlands out. These wastes—good for nothing more substantial—
Bloom light and outshine day. The lotus pond,
a repurposed wetland well south of its days,[1]
Is a perfect picture, empty, of the imperfection of your soul,
Helplessly in love with the vulgate particulars
of the secondhand world; in flower,

The pond is your Buddha self
at her ease; the Christ of St Thomas[2] come down
From the cross. Freedom starts, but refuses to stay, in want;
Literature takes its first steps in slur and slurry.
Put down roots where no one
Else can, in the compost of loss, in the suspect terrain
Of the only life you may ever get to grow in.
Nothing is wrong for long

And hope cannot stay lost,
if beauty can walk from the wreck,
And the lotus can raise heaven
from the dreck and the dross.

1 *well south of its days*: "South of My Days," Judith Wright.

2 *Christ of St Thomas*: the Cross of St Thomas features a lotus.

荷塘

給莎拉

如果你要天堂，就從淤泥起步吧。
　　　開始顯容吧，
就在你裹足不前的地方。你立足朝聖
泥濘上及腳踝。如果地面捆綁
　　　　　　如果靴子黏稠，如果你
脫靴而去，如果夏季
一天裏的香味，當池塘的水退去，就是惡臭
　　　　　　你起步的地方，就更純潔了。

當它們開花，你的想法就出現了
　　　當你呼吸，花園香味
更甜美了。當你最終決定開口說話
你的聲音更像鳥兒歌唱了。如果你要天空
　　　　　　就從水底起步吧。如果你要
照亮的大地，就從悲涼的地府起步吧，就從
那簇聽不見的耳朵起步吧。沉沒在腐壞之中，把種子
　　　撒播在紛爭之中，你的生命，每一個生命

都不時墮入其中：寧靜
　　　從骯髒中噴湧；愛是為愛，如果它
經受得住荒瘠之地。這些糟粕——一無是處——
盛放光芒，蓋過白日。這個荷塘
　　　　　　一片改變用途的濕地，它時日中的南方[1]
是一張完美的圖畫，空空的，畫中是你不完美的靈魂

無助地愛上了二手世界裏
　　　通行的細節。花開之時

荷塘就是你的佛陀自我
　　　她的自在。聖托馬斯基督從十字架上[2]
降臨。自由起步了，但是拒絕停下來，有所缺失
文學在污點和泥漿中踏出第一步
　　　　　　扎根於失去的有機肥料之中
沒有其他事物可以做到。在這可疑的地帶
唯一的生命可以讓你生長其中。
　　　沒有甚麼會錯得很久

希望也不會一直迷失，
　　　假若美麗可以走出頹唐
假若荷花可以從糟粕和浮渣中
　　　舉起天堂

（宋子江 譯）

1　「時日中的南方」語出澳洲詩人朱迪斯．萊特。
2　聖托馬斯的十字架樣子像荷花。

The Ugly

After John Glenday, "The Ugly"

The future refuses the past,
And the way
Things seem is rarely how things are. The present
Is a stranger to itself.
The plants go on
The best way they know how, being
Themselves as well as they can manage
In the changing face
of things, becoming
The world (each is born to be), each after
Its own fashion.

What we love in the one we love
Is the life
No one else knows how to live. Our love is how
We tend that gift
Which is hers alone.
And so, if I say I love her as I love the future
That unsettles everything I thought I knew,
I hope you'll understand.
I love her as time
Loves the *Welwitschia mirabilis*—after the corpse
Flower, the stinky squid,

The vegetable sheep, the fourth
Ugliest plant,
In botanical minds, in the world—who sets two leaves,
Once every two
Thousand years, and rolls them
Like ragged swags along the desert's floor, and thrives
In fabulous disarray so long
Under the Namibian
Sun, her leaves splitting
And sweeping themselves into a mess in a corner,
We may as well call it forever.

If your love lasts so long
They'll be calling it
A miracle. Find in your heart, then; find
In the heart of the one
You love, what grows nowhere
Else; love it, that stranger, as the wise learn
To love the Leafless Rockwattle;
The *acacia alata*
(var. Biglandulosa), that crowd
Of thorns; the green bird flower; the small-
Leaved Mottlecah,

A fallen altocumulus, her flowers
Like black holes
At a disco. Wander the world, a pilgrim of hard places;
Plumb your own deep north,
Your farthest west, and find there,
Where they prosper, the unconforming,
The wasted saints,
The scholars of the other
Way, the fallen dervishes, forever
Finding their two or three left feet again,
The addicts of the edge,

And see if you can find the future
In their ancient
Eyes, and in their image divine your days: the candel-
Abra aloe, burning sea-cliffs
Into ballrooms; the spiked cabbage
Tree, its leaves hors d'oeuvres for elephants,
Its roots a balm
To calm chaotic minds; *euphorbia ingens*,
A pot plant grown gargantuan
On the run; and the royal poinsiana, red carpet
For a canopy,
Its pea-green seeds faux canapes
For kingfishers
And dollarbirds, for princes and paupers and thieves,
To ignore,
Its leaves a sleepy tracery of summer
Dreams. How we contradict ourselves is who
We are; how we die to what
We'd hoped to be and rise again
Strange to ourselves as the future
To the past. Love is our work, whatever shape
It wants to take
In time

醜陋

擬約翰·格蘭地〈醜陋〉

未來拒絕往昔
而事物的方式
似乎很少一如所是。此刻
是自身的陌生人
植物繼起
它們知到最佳的方式，成為
它們自己，而且它們可以應付
事物改變的
面貌，成為
世界（各自天生），各自跟從
自身的裝束。

我們愛所愛者的
是生命
沒有人知道如何生活。我們的愛就是
如何照管她獨自的
禮物。
所以，如果我說我愛她，一如我愛未來
就會擾亂我以為自己所知的一切
我希望你會明白。
我愛她，一如時間
愛百歲蘭——在屍花、
紡錘佛手菌、

殘雪草之後，排名第四
最醜陋的植物
在植物學的頭腦中，在世間——百歲蘭開出兩片葉
每兩千年
一次，翻捲
一如沿著沙漠地表上的破爛行囊，長久地
在驚人的雜亂中茁壯成長
在納米比亞的日光
之下，她的葉子裂開
又自我捲成一角狼藉
我們也把它叫做永恆

如果你的愛曠日持久
他們會把它叫做
奇蹟。那麼，在你的內心尋找；在你所愛的人的
內心中尋找不在別處
生長的事物；愛它，那個陌生人一如智者學習
愛無葉的金合歡樹；
翅枝
金合歡，一堆
荊棘；綠鳥花；細葉
桉樹花，

墜落的高積雲，她的花
一如的士高裏的
黑洞。周遊世界，難行之地的朝聖者；
探測你自己的北部深處，
你西部最遠之處，到那裏尋找，
到他們繁盛的地方尋找，不隨俗
孱弱的聖者
另闢蹊徑的
學者，墮落的苦行僧，永遠
尷尷尬尬地站著
危險邊緣的入迷者，

然後看看你可否在他們
古老的眼睛裏
找到未來，或者從他們的形象猜測你的時日：南非
蘆薈，將海崖燃燒成
舞廳；穗狀花序的
澳洲朱蕉，葉子是大象的前菜，
它的根是香膏
鎮靜混亂的思緒；*燭台樹*，
忙個不停地
龐然生長的盆栽；鳳凰木，樹冠的
紅地毯，
青豆色種子，假的餐前薄餅
給翠鳥
和三寶鳥，給王子、窮人和盜賊
忽略了，
它的葉子是夏夢
睡意朦朧的窗花格。自相矛盾
我們正是如此；我們如此渴望
我們曾希望成為的自己，然後再次復活
對自己感到陌生，猶如往昔
之於未來。愛是我們的勞作，無論它
要以何種形態
存在於時光裏。

（鄭政恆 譯）

崔健（中國大陸），1961年出生於北京，被譽為「中國搖滾之父」。他是中國搖滾樂的先行者，也是最早親自創作歌詞的中國音樂人之一，其歌曲被一代又一代聽眾奉為經典。他出版的專輯包括《浪子歸》(1984)、《新長征路上的搖滾》(1989)、《解決》(1991)、《紅旗下的蛋》(1994)、《無能的力量》(1998)、《給你一點顏色》(2005)和《光凍》(2015)等。

Cui Jian (Mainland China), known as "The Father of Chinese Rock," was born in Beijing in 1961. A pioneer of Chinese rock music, he was one of the first Chinese musicians to write his own lyrics. His songs have become anthems to several generations of listeners. Among his albums are *Return of the Prodigal* (1984), *Rock 'n' Roll on the New Long March* (1989), *Solution* (1991), *Balls Under the Red Flag* (1994), *The Power of the Powerless* (1998), *Show You Colour* (2005), and *Frozen Light* (2015).

崔健

CUI JIAN

English translation by Canaan Morse

舞過三八線

雪天　雪地　雪花
它慢慢的不再刺激
北風吹進我的夢裏
我沒有醒　也沒有恐懼

藍天　草地　野花
它慢慢的失去了美麗
北風吹起了我醉意
我不願醒　也不願放棄

別問我為甚麼
別試著叫醒我
等我做完這個夢
等我唱完這首歌

Dancing Over the 38th Parallel

Snowfalls　snowscapes　snowflakes
The sting dies away in a while
North wind blows right into my dreams
I don't wake, but nor do I fear

Blue skies　green fields　flowers
Its charm dies away in a while
North wind stirring up my inebriation
I won't wake, nor will I give up

Don't ask me why or wherefore
Don't try to wake me up
Wait until I'm done with this dream
Wait until I've sung out this song

假行僧

我要從南走到北
我還要從白走到黑
我要人們都看到我
但不知道我是誰

假如你看我有點累
就請你給我倒碗水
假如你已經愛上我
就請你吻我的嘴

我有這雙腳　我有這雙腿
我有這千山和萬水
我要這所有的所有
但不要恨和悔

要愛上我就別怕後悔
總有一天我要遠走高飛
我不想留在一個地方
也不願有人跟隨

我要從南走到北
我還要從白走到黑
我要人們都看到我
但不知道我是誰

我只想看到你長得美
但不想知道你在受罪
我想要得到天上的水
但不是你的淚

我不願相信真的有魔鬼
也不願與任何人作對
你別想知道我到底是誰
也別想看到我的虛偽

嘞——

The Phony Traveling Monk

I walk the earth from low to high
I walk from black and into white
Everyone someday will see my face
But no one'll know my life

If you should see me weary grow
Come pour some water in my bowl
If you should fall in love with me
Then kiss me on my mouth

I've got my two legs and these two feet
Ten thousand hills and rivers deep
I want the whole of your everything
Except for regret and hate

In loving me, you can never hold on
I'll fly away and forever be gone
I gotta move and I never remain
And no one's coming along

I walk the earth from low to high
I walk from black and into white
Everyone someday will see my face
But no one'll know my life

Just want to see how pretty you look
Don't want to know 'bout the beating you took
Don't want no tears, just a heavenly spring
Whose water I may drink

I won't believe that devils exist
I'll never make any enemies
Forget about ever knowing who I am
Or finding my emptiness

Lei —

死不回頭

我站在浪尖風口
南牆碰了我的頭
我挺著身體背著手
風你可以斬我的首

廢話穿透了耳朵
恐懼壓歌喉
土地鬆軟沉默
骨頭變成了肉

我站在浪尖風口
南牆碰了我的頭
我挺著身體背著手
風你可以斬我的首

姑娘你跟在我身後
恐懼變憂愁
你是否還要跟我走
如果我死不回頭

南牆突然張開個口
要吃掉我的頭
它是否已經害怕我
知道我死不回頭

姑娘你跟在我身後
恐懼變憂愁
你是否還要跟我走
如果我死不回頭

誰讓我撞上了牆口
聞到了腐朽的臭
牆外到底是甚麼
等我把南牆撞透

Never Turning Back

I'm in the thick of it all
forehead hits the southern wall
I clasp my hands and stand up tall
Just cut my head, let it fall

Bullshit floats by my ears
Terror stops my throat
Soil is soft and silent
Bones transform into meat

I'm in the thick of it all
forehead hits the southern wall
I clasp my hands and stand up tall
Just cut my head, let it fall

Babe, when you're with me, all this fear
Turns to anxiety
Would you still want to follow me
If I swore not to turn back

The south wall opens up its mouth
To bite my head clean off
I bet it knows to be afraid
It knows I'm not turning back

Babe, when you're with me, all this fear
Turns to anxiety
Would you still want to follow me
If I swore not to turn back

So I just bashed all the bricks in
Smelled that sickening decay
Now what's on the other side
Wait till I bash my way through

一塊紅布

那天是你用一塊紅布
蒙住我雙眼也蒙住了天
你問我看見了甚麼
我説我看見了幸福

這個感覺真讓我舒服
它讓我忘掉我沒地兒住
你問我還要去何方
我説要上你的路

看不見你也看不見路
我的手也被你攥住
你問我在想甚麼
我説我要你做主

我感覺　你不是鐵
卻像鐵一樣強和烈
我感覺　你身上有血
因為你的手是熱乎乎

這個感覺真讓我舒服
讓我忘掉我沒地兒住
你問我還要去何方
我説要上你的路

我感覺　這不是荒野
卻看不見這地已經乾裂
我感覺　我要喝點水
可你的嘴將我的嘴堵住

我不能走我也不能哭
因為我身體已經乾枯
我要永遠這樣陪伴著你
因為我最知道你的痛苦

嘟……嘟……

A Strip of Red Cloth

That day you covered up my two eyes
Covered the sky with a strip of red cloth
And then you asked me what I saw
I told you I could see happiness

Oh this feeling is so positive
Makes me forget I've no place to live
You asked me where I want to go
I say I'm on the road to you

I can't see you, I can't see the road
My hand in your hand is tightly held
You ask me what I'm thinking of
I say I want you to take the lead

And though I feel   that you aren't steel
You're just as hard and sharp as steel can be
And I can tell   there's blood on your skin
It's heating up the hand my hand is in

Oh this feeling is so positive
Makes me forget I've no place to live
You asked me where I want to go
I say I'm on the road to you

And I can feel   this is no waste land
Yet I can't see the cracks in the ground
And now I feel   as dry as a drought
And yet your lips cover up my mouth

I cannot cry, and I cannot run
Because my body has all withered up
I want to stay with you forevermore
Because I understand your suffering

Doo— Doo—

周耀輝（香港），畢業於香港大學英國語文及比較文學系，其後參與多種媒體工作。1989 年發表第一首詞作，書寫歌詞及其他文字創作至今，出版約一千首詞作，以及文集《突然十年便過去》、《7749》、《假如我們甚麼都不怕》、《紙上染了藍》、《一個身體，兩個人》，曾獲多個詞作及其他文學獎項。1992 年移居荷蘭。2011 年獲阿姆斯特丹大學傳媒學院博士學位，回港任職浸會大學人文及創作系助理教授。近年亦參與舞台及視覺藝術創作。

Chow Yiu Fai (Hong Kong) has worked in many media. He has been writing song lyrics since his first publication in 1989, and by now they number upwards of 1,000. His books include *Suddenly, Decades Ago*, *7749: Forty-nine Exercises on Everyday Creativity*, *The Phobia Book*, *Blue Stained Paper*, and *One Body, Two People*. He moved to the Netherlands in 1992 and received a PhD in 2011 from the University of Amsterdam. Since returning to Hong Kong, he has taught as an assistant professor at Hong Kong Baptist University. His lyrics and writings have won numerous prizes.

周耀輝

CHOW YIU FAI

English translation by Lucas Klein and Chris Song

黑房

終於黑得可以沒時沒間
在右面或碰著誰人便吻吧
終於黑得一切狀態在雲集
在入面是一片熱巖能暴發

感官的張開　生死的掩蓋
我要你舌尖舔著我要害
有你　故我在
黑暗裏　永遠現在
光線裏　前塵又再

終於黑得可以沒人沒獸
第六步便發現誰人在背後
終於黑得一切動作沒遺漏
第十步是一撮引力而萬有

感官的張開　生死的掩蓋
我要你舌尖舔著我五內
有你　故我在
黑暗裏　永遠現在
光線裏　前塵又再

終於黑得可以沒言沒語
愈靜愈在煽動誰人亦錯亂
終於黑得一切陣線亦踰越
愈亂愈像一次革命難逆轉

感官的張開　生死的掩蓋
我要你舌尖舔著我實在
有你　故我在
黑暗裏　永遠現在
光線裏
前塵又再

Dark Room

It's so dark there's no more time or space
I can kiss whoever's here on my right
It's so dark all energy is a cloud
A blazing rock exploding inside

Senses whirl   Life and death unfurl
I want your tongue tip to lick my weakness
With you   therefore I am
In the dark   the eternal present
A ray of light   dust from the past

It's so dark there's no more man or beast
My sixth sense tells me who's behind me
It's so dark no move is unnoticed
The tenth step is the pull of gravity

Senses whirl   Life and death unfurl
I want your tongue tip to lick my insides
With you   therefore I am
In the dark   the eternal present
A ray of light   dust from the past

It's so dark there's no speech or sound
The quieter it gets the more agitation
It's so dark all lines are crossed
The more agitation the more like a revolution

Senses whirl   Life and death unfurl
I want your tongue tip to lick my immanence
With you   therefore I am
In the dark   the eternal present
A ray of light
dust from the past

下世紀再嬉戲

仍舊在辨認　漸漸淡的氣味
記起當天的鮮花會飛
遊玩在大地　漸漸再不顧忌
那曉得剎那轉了天氣

我記起跟你一起花裏遊戲
那笑聲多愉快多美
我記起跟你爭先吸一口氣
走過多芳香氣　奇妙世紀
到這天恐怕一切將要忘記
那記憶荒謬更淒美
到這天跟你一起不再頑皮
約定下世紀再嬉戲

Playing in the Next Century

I can still remember the scent lifting
that day the flowers were flying
We were loosened up playing on the ground
When the weather suddenly changed

I remember we were playing in the flowers
Our laughter so joyful and so sweet
we tried to take the first breath of it
How many fine scents　in this wonderful century
But that's all forgotten now
The more absurd our memories, the more painfully pretty
No more games or tricks
Until we're playing in the next century

雌雄同體

換了你皮膚
換了你唇舌
換了你全身的感覺　即刻識穿我希望
換了你是我
亦發覺連心思都有　女或男
我跟你相差多不多

我的香煙　借給你抽兩天
然後期望你心裏就有我的事
或者會變性　當我接近你一點
你的新衣　借給我穿兩天
難道要換性別　至得到你體驗
寧願接近到　當你詫異　伸我舌尖

換了我瞳孔
換了我頭髮
換了我無色的香氣　即刻棲身你天地
換了我是你
亦發覺連瘋癲都有　女或男
我們卻偏偏想一起

你的高踭　借給我踩兩天
然後期望我心裏就有你的事
或者會變性　當你接近我一點
我的鬚根　借給你穿兩天
難道要換性別　至參透你思念
寧願接近到　不靠說話也知

我的香煙　借給你抽兩天
然後期望你心裏就有我的事
或者會變性　當我接近你一點
你的新衣　借給我穿兩天
難道要換性別　至得到你體驗
寧願接近到　當你快樂　我會癲

也許只有迷戀會叫我改變
我要變做你　將命運亦重疊

Androgyny

You wear my skin
You take my lips and tongue
You feel my body   and you'll see through my hopes
If you were me
You'd you get my thoughts   Female or male
How different am I from you?

Take my cigarettes   smoke for two days
I hope you'll inhale my thoughts
Or change sex   When I come a little closer
I take your clothes   and wear them for two days
Do I have to change my sex   before I feel what you feel
I'd rather get closer   when you're in shock   you stretch out my tongue

I have your pupils
I have your hair
I have your colorless scent   I'll dwell in your world
If I were you
I'd find I had your madness   Female or male
Wouldn't they be better as one

Lend me your high heels   I'll wear them for two days
And hope I'll get your thoughts
Or change sex   When you come a little closer
Take my stubble   don't shave for two days
Do you have to change your sex   before you feel what I feel
I'd rather get closer   so we can know without having to speak

Take my cigarettes   smoke for two days
I hope you'll inhale my thoughts
Or change sex   When I come a little closer
I take your clothes   and wear them for two days
Do I have to change my sex   before I feel what you feel
I'd rather get closer   when you're happy   and I can go crazy

maybe only obsession will make me change
I want to be you   our fates superimposed

如髮

至少可以不害怕
至少可以跟誰回家
將建立過他還塌陷過她
是否自由　極之像貪
至少可以不害怕
陪他呼吸她喜歡嗎
當一切完成後　快樂嗎

前身鋪於每次事後
眾生歸於一些滲透
如汗彎彎彎到　雙腳之間

暗暗生出如髮　濃濃密密似掛於心眼裏的麻
暗暗生出幼嫩的黑　濃濃密密像萬句某異國的説話
沾濕過最後為蒸發
能填盡萬個裏海未能填盡我空白
濃濃密密像沒有面孔的面紗
暗暗生出如髮
濃濃密密似散於肌膚裏的繁華
細碎紛亂偶然生出造化
吻過天下成就我一束　黑髮

前身鋪於每次事後
眾生歸於一些滲透
奇妙也就莫名　必須呼喊它　是愛嗎

暗暗生出如髮　濃濃密密似掛於心眼裏的麻
暗暗生出幼嫩的黑　濃濃密密像萬句某異國的説話
沾濕過最後為蒸發
能填盡萬個裏海未能填盡我空白
濃濃密密像沒有面孔的面紗
暗暗生出如髮
濃濃密密似散於十剎盡處的天下
春風過最後又再生
生於荒原延續到腳下　在情慾之間
吻過天下難道愛只得片刻

將一串雨露變做我袈裟
將一塊碎石當做我釋迦
不歸路上等稀客
我是誰　能行在野地
跪在野花
最後亦能一身只有雪花

永遠生出如髮
永遠生出幼嫩的黑
沾濕過最後為蒸發
能填盡萬個裏海未能填盡我空白
濃濃密密似愛嗎
世界生出如髮
濃濃密密似散於六尺善惡的真假
春風過最後又再生生於當前情願不説話
吻過天下除下我　一身黑髮
吻過天下遺下了
遍地紅顏

Like Hair

At least I don't have to be afraid
At least I can come home with somebody
Building him up or crashing her down
Am I free　So much like greed
At least I don't have to be afraid
Does she like breathing with him?
After it's all done　is she happy?

I lie down after every time
All life comes down to osmosis
Like sweat dripping and dripping down　between our feet

It grows dark like hair　dense like twisting flax in the mind
It grows dark and tender black　dense like a million words in a foreign tongue
Drenched only to evaporate
It will fill ten thousand seas but not fill up my emptiness
Dense like a veil without a face
It grows dark like hair
Dense like a flourishing on the skin
Bits and pieces growing into all creation
Kissing the whole world to accomplish a lock　of black hair

I lie down after every time
All life comes down to osmosis
Wonderful and ineffable   but I must shout it out   Is it love?

It grows dark like hair   dense like twisting flax in the mind
It grows dark and tender black   dense like a million words in a foreign tongue
It soaks to evaporate   it fills ten thousand seas but not where I'm hollow
It grows dark like hair   dense like a veil that has no face to cover
Dense like a world splintered into ten distant temples
Spring winds blow past and it's growing yet again
Growing in a waste land stretching to our feet   in desire
Kissing the whole world just for a moment of love?

A string of rain dews to be my Kāṣāya
A piece of rock to be my Śākya
At the point of no return   I wait for passersby
Who am I   to walk in the wild?
To kneel on wild flowers
And to be covered in snow

Forever it grows like hair
Forever it grows tender and black
Drenched only to evaporate
It will fill ten thousand seas but not fill up my emptiness
Is it as dense as love
The world grows like hair
Dense like real and fake splintered to six inches of good and evil
Spring winds blow past and it's growing yet again growing when we'd
    rather not speak
Kissing the whole world just to leave me behind   all my black hair
Kissing the whole world just to leave me
rouge affairs

傑閎・格庵（法國），跨界創作人，1971 年生於法國巴黎，旅居巴黎與紐約兩地。著作超過二十本，曾出版有聲詩 CD 以及影像詩 DVD，在法國及世界各地作公開演出，與視覺藝術家、音樂家、舞台導演和編舞師進行跨界合作。著有數本關於當代美學的文集。2015 年在摩洛哥卡薩布蘭卡進行第一次個展。他的詩作有中文、日文、英文、西班牙文、意大利文等譯本。2017 年，倫敦 Barque 出版社將出版他的英譯詩集*Flip-Book & Other Image-Poems*。

Jérôme Game (France), born in Paris in 1971, has been based in between Paris and New York City over the last few years. Since 2000 he has published over twenty books, several CDs (of sound-poetry), one DVD (of videopoems), and given numerous public performances of his work in France and abroad (Europe, North Africa, Asia, Americas). Translation, correspondence, appropriation: it is across various practices and disciplinary borders that his poetry recomposes, often in collaborations with visual artists, musicians, stage directors and choreographers. He has also published several essays on contemporary aesthetics and had his first exhibition in 2015 in Casablanca, Morocco. His poems have been translated into several languages (English, Spanish, Italian, Chinese, Japanese) and later in 2017 *Flip-Book & Other Image-Poems*, a collection of English translations, will come out with Barque Press in London.

傑閎・格庵

JÉRÔME GAME

中文翻譯：翁文嫻

English Translation by François Luong

HK Live!

HongK c'est HongK ong c'est

Pour les articles homon hom, voir HongK voir hom

c'est 22 degrés 16 min. 42 sec. Nnord / 114 degrés
9 min. 32 sec. Eest

La c, voir la c

C'est chin contient des caractères chin, c'est en chinois, littéralement « parfum aux fleurs », « port aux fleurs », ça veut dire « des fleurs ». En cant en cantonnais : Hēung Góng *Hē-ung-góng.*

Hong Kong Special Administrative Region Administ est la plus grande est la plus peuplée des deux Régions Admini des Régions Spéciales de l'autre étant, l'autre étant Mac

Elle compte environ 7 millions est située sur la Rive orientale sur la Côté sud est baignée par la mer éridionale.
Au nord : Guangdong
Au sud : la mer

Gouvernement : chef du Donald Donald Tsang

Supererficie : 1104 km ca onze cent quatre km^2
7 018 636 habitants

63se 637 6.357 habitants au km^2 mais en fait 30.000 si on tient si l'on tient compte de la densité des montagnes du relief moyen escarpé

Le cantonnais, l'anglais, le *cash*
le pôle financier le PIB
254 milliards 200 millions de dollars
dollars chinois, 38.127 par an par habitant

Le pays aux deux systèmes : sa monnaie, son système légal, ses équipes sportives internationales, son système policier, ses lois sur l'immigration jusqu'en 2047, soit 50 ans après la réintég

Bon.
C'est le transfert
c'est la région du delta
c'est montagneux
c'est les Britanniques c'est
la Rétrocession c'est
les Nouveaux Territoires
le Pic Victoria
la Tai Mo Shan
le climat, les colons, les lois, les bon mais
C'est comment parler de
la 3ème place la 1ère en densité la 11ème entité comment ça ? le 8ème du monde, les plus bas, par tonnage cargo, 260.700.000 tonnes métriques, le 3ème

24.650.000 conteneurs traités, le boom, l'air saturé, la concentration, la densité, l'exode, commencent à refluer, a commencé, concurrencé, demeure la 1ère en devises étrangères, bon mais alors qu'est est-ce que c'est qu

Bon.

- 1 Géographie
  - 1.1 L'île de Hong Kong et Kowloon
  - 1.2 Les Nouveaux Territoires
  - 1.3 Climat

- 2 Histoire
  - 2.1 La première colonisation anglaise
  - 2.2 La colonie anglaise pendant la période communiste
  - 2.3 La rétrocession à la Chine

- 3 Organisation politique, judiciaire et administrative
  - 3.1 Système politique
  - 3.2 Système juridique
  - 3.3 Découpage administratif et politique

- 4 Transports
  - 4.1 Transports ferroviaires
  - 4.2 Transports routiers
  - 4.3 Transports maritimes
  - 4.4 Transports aériens

- 5 Économie
  - 5.1 La tertiarisation
  - 5.2 Une économie tournée vers l'extérieur
  - 5.3 Les concurrents

- 6 Démographie

- 7 Culture
  - 7.1 Langues
  - 7.2 Enseignement supérieur
  - 7.3 Sport
  - 7.4 Architecture

- 8 Religions
- 9 Natifs de Hong Kong
- 10 Codes
- 11 Notes et références

- 12 Voir aussi
  - 12.1 Articles connexes
  - 12.2 Liens externes

Et puis Hong Kong c'est aussi c'est encore les stars, Hong Kong et ses célébrités. Stars de Hong Kong:

- René de Obaldia
- Andy Lau
- Chow Yun-fat
- Jackie Chan
- Amanda Lear
- Leung Guo-Hung
- Tony Leung Chiu-wai
- Maggie Cheung
- Ma Ying-jeou
- Nicholas Tse
- Stephen Chow
- Jiro Wang
- Niki Chow
- Kelly Chen
- Johnnie To
- Wong Kar-Waï

C'est comme un Wiki, non ? C'est comme un
portrait-robot
de la ville
sur la carte
à l'écran.

Qu'est-ce qu'on voit ?

Ça zoome on dirait ça grossit, on se rapproche.
On voit c'est marron bleu foncé, ça avance lentement, c'est gris.
Qu'est-ce qu'on voit ?

On voit Tsim Sha Tsui, le point le port, le tunnel par en-dessous, Victoria. On voit Shang Wan, Admiralty, on voit Central, Causeway Bay, l'hôpital, Wan Chaï.

C'est foncé, c'est l'eau, ça s'éclaircit un peu en zoomant, c'est la nuit aussi c'est le jour. On a traversé les nuages cependant, on zoome, les gens bougent, tous les chats sont gris. *Kwoloon, Lantau, Stanley Village, Union Square. On est en géostation, on lévite, on voit l'ombre par en-dessous la lumière à midi, à 100 mètres au-dessus des buildings. Il fait frais, le ciel est clair. Le court de tennis sur le toit de l'International Commerce Center, le Ritz Carlton et les bureaux, la plateforme panoramique et les touristes au 100*ème *étage sur la terrace du Twin International Finance Center, le Central Plazza, la Bank of China. C'est I.M. Pei, c'est Foster, c'est Richard Rogers, Cesar Pelli, c'est Rem Koolhaas.* L'écran bouge, tilte un peu. Les bouches d'aération la ventilation, les pales, la fumée vue de haut. C'est orthonormé, c'est rond dans les carrés, en losanges bien calés, ça s'agence, ça se tient bien serré c'est rempli. Y'en a partout, c'est super-dense, ça a tout recouvert.

Le court de tennis est bleu, les ombres turquoises, on voit les toits ombrés, la végétation les ruelles, les voitures sont garées, les rues défilent en biais, *le plan du robot le satellite orbite fait glisser l'écran à travers* le bleu vert est clair, pixellisé. Le rouge de Sienne délavé, le stade en terre battue le vert bouteille des toits en taule plissée, le satellite tressaute, repart dans l'autre sens, il change de côté. *L'usine, le parking, les clous sur la chaussée, les emplacements vides pour se garer, les traits blancs sur gris foncé. Il y a de l'air, c'est l'hiver, de la lumière. Il remonte vers la gare, on voit le marquage au sol blanc, les lignes de chemins de fer la rouille sont dans les ocres, les toits blancs-gris une voiture rouge c'est plus lent, ça ralentit.* L'avenue repart vers la mer, le bitume s'éclaircit. Le jaune, le marron clair, ça se dé-densifie. Les pontons, les quais s'alignent en biais le bleu s'enfonce, les bateaux, la lumière sur l'eau fripée le port, le pont pixellisé on remonte. Le satellite rem reprend du champ de la hauteur. La surface de l'océan devient béton, s'assombrit. En bas la plage, les pontons des villas de Stanley les estivants, le yacht est arrivé.

*

“Bons bons baisers de...” Bons baisers de...

On on est où là ? Ça donne quoi ?

ça donne oui oui, ça s’écrit comme ça comme sans aspérité, comme une *postc* ard en arrière, comme en écoutant du chinois, trois pattes-de-mouche jetées là, un *snapshot*, une esquisse, un sketch, un schéma, une ébauche, une amorce, un canev un canevas a un croquis, une idée, un début, un essai, un germe, un squelette, une maquette, un premier jet, un projet, un topo, un crayon, un crayon

On voit les choses cadrées, un peu de verdure à l’angle supérieur droit. La postcard est vernie «*Bons baisers*»,
gentils chinois, jonques en bois, chapeaux pointus, avenues en perspective, tables garnies, noms de, autobus à impériale, noms de rue :

- Clouded View Road

- North Point Road

- Electric Road

- Oil Road

- Blue Pool Road

- Gage Street

- Peel Street

- Le High Court Building

- L’Old Supreme Court Building

- Le Battery Path

- Le French Mission Building

- Le St-John’s Cathedral

- Le Government House

- L’Old Dairy Farm Building

- Le Bishop’s House

- Le HSBC Main Building

- Le Hong Kong Park

- Le Kowloon Park

- Le Happy Valley

Mais alors ça déborde aussi, ça grossit là, les photos, le cadre. Qu'est-ce qu'on voit ?

On voit *elliptic loop of sens of sensations and of smells and of always the same : lemongrass, jasmin-tea, snapshots or postcards* attachées en liasses comme ça. On a : "Bons, bons baisers d'bons baisers de… » On est où là ? Ça donne quoi en phot en photo ?

香港現場！

香港是香港
是
有關這通通一模一樣書寫唉，看香K　唉
看北緯22度16分42秒/
東經
114度9分32秒

這有C，要看C

是chin包括這些chin的字母，
是中文，字形字義「花香」，「花的港口」，即是說「許多花」。
用廣東話：*Hē-ung-góng.*

香港特別行政區是最大人口最多在兩個特別行政區言，另一個是澳門

她差不多七百萬座落東海岸旁邊沐浴在南中國海。
以北：廣東
以南：海

政府：唐老鴨主人　曾蔭權(Donald Tsang)
地表面積：阿拉伯數字1104一千一百零四平方公里
7018636
居民
63自變成637　6.357居民在每一平方公里但事實上是
30.000若我們考慮

考慮山勢的
陡峭起伏的密度

廣東人，英國人，*現金*
金融熱點
百科全書
2540 億加200 個百萬
人民幣，每年38.127
每位居民

一國兩制：貨幣，律法，國際運動團隊，警察，移民法律直至
2047 年，或
回歸之後
50 年

好。這是
轉移
這是
三角洲流域這是
群山起伏
這是英國人
這是回歸這是
新界
維多利亞
大帽山

氣候、駐軍、法令、證券
但如何說關於
世界第三位密度第一位如何說第十一位的
實體呢？世界第八，是最
低的，在貨運吞吐量，
260.200.000 *公噸，第三位*
24.650.000 *貨櫃合約，暴漲繁榮，過飽和*
中央集權，密度，出走移民，開始
回流，再開始，競爭，維持
外匯第一名，很好但究竟
這究竟是甚麼

好。

1. 地理
    - 1.1 香港島與九龍
    - 1.2 新界
    - 1.3 氣候

2. 歷史
    - 2.1 第一個英國殖民地
    - 2.2 在共產黨政權時期的英國殖民地
    - 2.3 回歸中國

3. 政治、法律與行政組織

- 3.1 政治制度
- 3.2 法律制度
- 3.3 政治與行政的切割

4. 交通
    - 4.1 鐵路交通
    - 4.2 公路交通
    - 4.3 海上交通
    - 4.4 航空交通

5. 經濟
    - 5.1 第三產業化
    - 5.2 外向型經濟
    - 5.3 競爭對手

6. 人口統計學

7. 文化
    - 7.1 語言
    - 7.2 高等教育
    - 7.3 體育
    - 7.4 建築

8. 宗教
9. 香港本土居民

10. 守則
11. 附註與參考

12. 更多閱讀資源
    - 12.1 相關的問題
    - 12.2 外緣關係

於是香港仍如是仍是明星們，
香港與她的名流。香港明星：

- 藍尼奧巴第[1]
- 劉德華
- 周潤發
- 成龍
- 阿曼達．麗兒[2]
- 梁國雄
- 梁朝偉
- 張曼玉
- 馬英九[3]
- 謝霆鋒

1 譯註：René de obaldia 法國作家，1918 年生於香港，有32 本詩、小說及戲劇著作。1999 年受聘為法蘭西院士。最著名為《擦樹枝條上的風》(*Le vent dans les branches de Sassafras*)。

2 譯註：Amanda Lear ，1950 年出生於香港，法國歌手。

3 譯註：1950 年出生於香港。

。周星馳
。汪東城
。周麗淇
。陳慧琳
。杜琪峯
。王家衛

這如維基百科？不是嗎？這
如機器製造的影像
在城市
地圖的
螢光幕上

究竟甚麼是我們看見？

焦點變化時我們說愈來愈大，我們
接近它
看見深藍栗色，向前
慢慢地，是灰色。
究竟甚麼是我們看見？

看見尖沙咀，海港的尖點，而
隧道在下面，維多利亞。看見上
環，金鐘，看見中環，銅鑼灣，

醫院，灣仔。

是深色，是水，會明亮些些在
變焦鏡頭下，是晚上也是白天。然而我們
穿過雲，變焦，那些
人移動，所有的貓灰色。*九龍*
大嶼山，赤柱，聯合廣場。我們
在衛星導航，我們靈視升空，我們看見

*陰影在中午光線的下面，在建築物一百碼的上面。天氣涼，天空明亮。國際商業大樓屋頂的網球場，麗思卡尼頓酒店及辦公室，全視景月台遊客們在一百樓環球貿易廣場的平台上，中區廣場，中國銀行。是貝聿銘，是雷姆庫哈斯[4]，銀幕移動，有點兒傾斜。*那些換氣通風孔道，那些蒼白黯淡，那些高處的煙。總是一板一眼的，四方體裝圓形，菱形要好好墊穩，全裝備安排好，一切緊靠填滿。到處都如此，超級稠密，全部重新覆蓋。

網球場是藍色的，陰影是土耳其綠，我們看見屋頂陰影，小巷如植物的生長，那些車全部停放好，小街歪斜著魚貫前行，*機器的地圖衛星航道將銀幕滑移至藍綠明亮色*，畫素更清晰。濃妝豔抹的塞納河褪淡了，運動場土地攪著綠瓶子瓦面屋頂起皺，衛星驚跳，重新

4　譯註：Rem Koolhaas，荷蘭建築師，生於1944年。

向另一面出發，方位改了。*工廠，停車場，最精彩部份在堤岸，有空的場地等停車，深灰上白色的線條。這兒有流動的風，是冬天，的光線。再爬上車站，我們看見白地上的記號，鐵路的軌跡將它銹成赭石色，灰白的屋頂間一輛紅車是更慢，更放鬆。*大道再次開向海，柏油路愈來愈亮。黃色、淺栗色，會減低密度。沿著一排排浮橋，海堤斜斜地加深了藍色，那些船，水上的光將港口弄皺，我們再度登上畫素清晰的橋。衛星偵測再度升高。海洋的表面變成水泥，變暗變憂鬱。海灘下面，赤柱村的浮台度假者，遊艇已經來了。

*

「快樂快樂的吻是……」「快樂的吻是……」

我們在哪兒呢？這算是？

是的這會是，寫成這樣有如沒有凹凸不平的地表，有如明信片的背面，有如我們聽著中文，幾個潦草小字丟在哪兒，一張快照，一個滑稽短劇，一個提綱，一張草圖，一個片頭，一些草稿中的要點，一些想法，一個開場，一種嘗試，一種醞釀萌芽，一個骨架，一個模型，一口氣寫下的，一種構想，一個介紹，一個素描一個素描。

我們看見裝裱過的事物，在筆直角度上小小的綠色。明信片光亮漆上*「快樂的吻」*，親切的中文字，木艇船家，尖尖的帽，光輝繁榮的大道，擺滿的餐桌，名字是，英皇御准公車，路名：

—雲景道

—北角道

—電氣道

—油街

—藍塘道

—結志街

—卑利街

—高等法院大樓

—終審法院大樓

—炮台山

—法國外方傳道會大樓

—聖約翰座堂

—禮賓府

—舊牛奶公司倉庫

—會督府

—香港上海匯豐銀行大廈

—香港公園

—九龍公園

—跑馬地

嗯但這是滿出來了，太誇張了，這些照片，框架。我們究竟看到甚麼？

*看見簡略的一捆意義一紮感官與味道與及總是一樣的：檸檬香茅，茉莉花茶，快拍或明信片*紮成一捆。我們有：「快樂，快樂的吻來自快樂的吻來自……」我們在哪兒呢？照片上照出些甚麼？

HK Live!

HongK this is Hongk ong this

For oth other use uses, see HongK see oth

It's 22 degrees 16 min. 42 sec. Nnorth / 114 degrees 9 min. 32 sec. Eeast

The c, see the c

It's in Chin contains Chin characters, it's in Chinese, literally "flagrance of flowers," "fragrant harbor," it means "of flowers." In Cant in Cantonese: Hēung Góng *Hē-ung-góng.*

Hong Kong Special Administrative Region Administ is the largest is the most populated of the two Admini Regions of the Special Regions of the other being, the other being Mac

It has about 7 millions is located on the on the Eastern Shore on the South Side is washed the outh Sea.
To the North: Guangdong
To the South: the sea

Government: head of Donald Donald Tsang

Area: 1104 squa km eleven hundre four km2 7 018 636 inhabitants
63se 637 6 357 inhabitants per km2 but actually 30 000 if

we take if we take into account the density mountains with an average steep relief

Cantonese, English, *cash*
financial hub, GDP
254 billion 200 million dollars
Chinese dollars, 38 127 per year per inhabitant

A country with two systems: its currency, its legal system, its international sports teams, its police system, its immigration laws until 2047, or 50 years after reinteg

Well.
This is the transfer
this is the delta region
this is mountainous
this is the British this is
the Handover this is
the New Territories
Victoria Peak
Tai Mo Shan
the climate, the settlers, the laws, the yes but
This how to speak of
the third place the first in density the 11th entity what's that? the 8th in the world, the lowest, by cargo tonnage, 260 700 000 metric tons, the 3rd 24 650 000 containers handled, the book, the saturated air, the concentration, the density, the exodus, start to decline, has started, challenged, remains the 1st for foreign currencies, well but then what is it wh

Well.

- 1 Geography
  - 1.1 Hong Kong Island and Kowloon
  - 1.2 The New Territories
  - 1.3 Climate

- 2 History
  - 2.1 First English settlement
  - 2.2 The English colony during the Communist era
  - 2.3 Handover to China

- 3 Political, judicial and administrative organization
  - 3.1 Political organization
  - 3.2 Judicial organization
  - 3.3 Administrative and political regions

- 4 Transport
  - 4.1 Rail transport
  - 4.2 Road transport

    - 4.3 Maritime transport
    - 4.4 Air transport

- 5 Economy
    - 5.1 Service economy
    - 5.2 An outward-looking economy
    - 5.3 Competitors

- 6 Demography

- 7 Culture
    - 7.1 Languages
    - 7.2 Higher education
    - 7.3 Sports
    - 7.4 Architecture

- 8 Religions
- 9 Hong Kong natives
- 10 Codes
- 11 Notes and references

- 12 Further reading
    - 12.1 Related articles
    - 12.2 External links

And so Hong Kong it's also it's still the stars. Hong Kong and its stars. Stars of Hong Kong:

- René de Obaldia
- Andy Lau
- Chow Yun-fat
- Jackie Chan
- Amanda Lear
- Leung Kwok Hung
- Tony Leung Chiu-wai
- Maggie Cheung
- Ma Ying-jeou
- Nicholas Tse
- Stephen Chow
- Jiro Wang
- Niki Chow
- Kelly Chen
- Johnnie To
- Wong Kar-Wai

It's a bit like a Wiki, isn't it? It's a bit like a composite portrait
of the city
on the map
on the screen

What do you see?

It zooms it looks like it grows, we get closer.
We see it's a dark blue maroon, it moves slowly, it's grey
What do you see?

We see Tsim Sha Tsui, the dot the port, the tunnel underneath, Victoria. We see Shang Wan, Admiralty, we see Central, Causeway Bay, the hospital, Wan Chai.

It's dark, it's water. it brightens a bit when we zoom, it's night too it's day. We've gone through clouds however, we zoom, people move, every cat is grey. *Kwoloon, Lantau, Stanley Village, Union Square. We're in geostationary orbit, we float, we see the shadow underneath the light at noon, at 100 meters above the buildings. The air is fresh, the sky is clear. The tennis court on the roof of the International Commerce Center, the Ritz Carlton and the offices, the viewing platform and tourists on the 100th floor on the terrace of the Twin International Finance Center, the Central Plazza, the Bank of China. It's I. M. Pei, it's Foster, it's Richard Rogers, Cesar Pelli, it's Rem Koolhaas.* The screen moves, it tilts a bit. The air vents the ventilation, the blades, the smoke seen from above. It's orthonormal, it's round like in squares, in diamonds properly set, it moves around, it stands quite tightly it's full. It's everywhere, it's so very dense, it has covered everything.

The tennis court is blue, the shadows turquoise, we see shaded roofs, the vegetations the alleys, the cars are parked, the streets run at an angle, *the robot's plan the satellite orbits slides the screen through* the blue green is clear, pixelated. The sienna red is washed out, the dirt-floor stadium the bottle green of the pleated sheet-metal roofs, the satellite staggers, goes the other way, it changes sides. *The factory, the parking lot, zebra lines on the crossing, the empty spots to park, the white lines on dark grey. There is air, it's winter, light. He goes back to the train station, you see the white road markings, the railroad lines rust are in the ochers, the white-grey roofs a red car it's slower, it slows down.* The avenue returns to the sea, the pavement brightens. Yellow, light maroon, it un-densifies. The piers, the wharves line up at an angle the blue sinks, the boats, the disheveled light on the water the port the pixelated bridge we rise back. The satellite ris regains field height. The surface of the ocean becomes concrete, darkens. Below the beach, the piers villas in Stanley summer visitors, the yacht has arrived.

*

"Greet greetings from…" Greetings from…

Where where are we now? How's it going?

it goes yes yes, this is how it's written like this like smoothly like a *postc* ard in the back, like listening to Chinese, three black scrawlings thrown there, a *snapshot*, a draft, a sketch, a diagram, a rough, a primer, a canv a canvas as a drawing, an idea, a start, an essay, a sprout, a skeleton, a model, a first draft, a project, a brief, a pencil, a pencil

We see things framed, a bit of greenery on the top right angle. The postcard is varnished "*Greetings*," nice Chinese, wooden junk, pointed hats, avenues in perspective, garnished tables, names of, double-decker bus, names of streets:

- Clouded View Road

- North Point Road

- Electric Road

- Oil Street

- Blue Pool Road

- Gage Street
- Peel Street
- The High Court Building
- The Old Supreme Court Building
- Battery Path
- The French Mission Building
- St. John's Cathedral
- The Government House
- The Old Dairy Farm Building
- Bishop's House
- The HSBC Main Building
- Hong Kong Park
- The Happy Valley

And so it overflows too, it grows there, the photos, the frame. What do you see?

We see *elliptic loop of sens of sensations and of smells and of always the same: lemongrass, jasmin-tea, snapshots or postcards* attached in bundles like this. We have: "Greet, greeting fr greetings from…" Where are we now? How is it going as a phot as a photo?

查爾斯．伯恩斯坦（美國）最近出版的詩集有 *Pitch of Poetry*（芝加哥大學出版社，2016）及 *Recalculating*（芝加哥大學出版社，2013）。2010 年 Farrar, Straus & Giroux 出版社出版了他的詩選集 *All the Whiskey in Heaven: Selected Poems*。有兩本詩集被譯為中文：《L=A=N=G=U=A=G=E POETICS》（羅良功等譯，上海外語教育出版社，2013）及《查爾斯．伯恩斯坦詩選》(聶珍釗、羅良功等譯，譯林出版社，2010；華中師範大學出版社，2011)。2015 年獲 Münster 國際詩歌獎和 Janus Pannonius 詩歌大獎。現於賓夕法尼亞大學任教，為該校 Donald T. Tegan 英文及比較文學教授。現為中美詩歌與詩學協會副主席、美國文理科學院院士。

Charles Bernstein (USA) is the author of *Pitch of Poetry* (University of Chicago Press, 2016) and *Recalculating* (University of Chicago Press, 2013). In 2010, Farrar, Straus & Giroux published *All the Whiskey in Heaven: Selected Poems*. He is vice-president of the Chinese American Association of Poetry and Poetics (CAAP). He has two books in Chinese translation: *L=A=N=G=U=A=G=E POETICS*, translated by Luo Lianggong and others (Shanghai Foreign Language Education Press, China, 2013) and *Selected Poems* translated by Nie Zhenzhao and Luo Lianggong (first edition in Nanjing: Yilin Press, 2010; second edition in Wuhan, Central China Normal University Press, 2011). Bernstein is Donald T. Regan Professor of English and Comparative Literature at the University of Pennsylvania. In 2015 Bernstein was awarded both the Münster Prize for International Poetry and Janus Pannonius Grand Prize for Poetry. He is a Fellow of the American Academy of Arts and Sciences.

查爾斯・伯恩斯坦

CHARLES BERNSTEIN

中文翻譯：黎志敏

Pinky's Rule

It always starts
fast then begins
unwinding.
A relatively
straight shot
right to the
moon (in freeze
frame):
as if you're
almost at the
point of being
nearly ready.
Abrupt shift
as in I'll
catch you
next time, wipe
that stare off
your filmy
inconsequence,
give me a
rain dance, a
walk around the
projected parking
structure,
my indubitable
loquacity, the
ice machine next
to the ice
truck, Sunday
morning chill.
Mellow the way a
lemon calls out your
name in the dark,
only it's saying "Alice"
and your name is
John, or then it's
saying "Paulo"
but you hear
it as *hollow*.
Instrumental,
that is, only in
the name I
find when the
shooting's over
and the bed linen's
on the line.
It comes to this
or it came to that
or I shouldda
listened harder or
I heard too much.
Just don't bet the

ranch on the chance
your horse will come
in second. There is
no place like
a blue pipe on a
blunt background:
that would be a
pony of a different
stripe. Heaven doesn't
ask and won't tell.
Here on the ground
you have to make
a lot of guesses, but
even the most astute
hunch don't
change the course
of all you've tried
to push against.
The fuel's not so much
finite as tainted. Perception
bows to the low-person
on totem's pole.
Or forms a filter
against chance
encounters, meteoric
ineptitude, undeniable
resemblances. You
don't got to be
Plato to see the
shadows on the wall.
Going where
you think you
go, coming from
wherever
you thought you'd
come from.
I go in fear of
fear but on the
flip side of
the coin, early
risers cut short
the night. Illusion
is always 9/10ths
collusion and half
wistful thinking.
Take another look:
there is no more
collateral damage
to that thought
than to the beach
when the wave
breaks over it.

The picture can
say only what
the words tell
it not to, as in
the pope is
in the silo
while the poetry
boy redoubles
his and her
effortlessness.
It's a running
dope, or more
kind to say,
inept propositional.
Where did you
say you put
the pliers?
She's only this
far from destiny.
But they only sell
one-way tickets.
The warp of the weft
is beset by fits.
And then it comes
to pass that the oblong
is covered in shadow.

As long as you
both shall spill.

Pinkies rule.
This is what
she told me.

小指頭的統治

開始時總是
急，然後
鬆懈。
這一下子
較為直率
直擊月亮（在
定格的鏡頭中）：
似乎你
總是處於
幾乎準備好了的狀態。
突然轉移
就像說
下次我會
抓住你，
將你眼神中
朦朧的輕視
擦乾淨，
給我跳個
祈雨舞，
繞著規劃的
停車場
散步，
我無可置疑的
煩言碎語，
載冰卡車旁的
造冰機器

星期天早晨的
寒冷。
檸檬在黑暗中
喊你的名字
那麼柔和，
它喊著「愛麗絲」
可你的名字是
「約翰」，然後它說
「鯤鵬」
可是你聽成了
「*空洞*」。
驚人地發現
只是在我
發現的
名字中，當射擊
已經完成時
當床上的床單
晾曬在繩子上時。
這樣或者
那樣或者
我本來應該
聽得更努力一些
或者我聽得太多了。
可別孤注一擲
你的馬可能

會得第二。
沒有甚麼地方
像淺露背景中
的一隻藍色管子：
那會是一匹不同
條紋的矮種馬。
上天不會問
也不會説。
在大地上
你不得不做出
很多猜測，但是
即便最機警的
直覺也無法
改變你一直努力
反對的事件
的運行軌跡。
燃料不是有限
而是已經污染了。
洞察向圖騰柱
最底層的人鞠躬。
或許可以
避免偶然的
不期而遇，眼花繚亂的
笨拙，不可否認的
相似。你
不必一定要成為
柏拉圖才能看見
牆上的陰影。
想到哪兒去，
就到哪兒去
你覺得你
是從哪兒來
你就是
從哪兒來的。
我害怕害怕，
可是反過來説
早起的人們
切短了夜晚。
幻覺總是
十分之九的
勾結與一半
熱切的思考。
再看一眼：
那個想法的
附帶損害
並不比海浪
襲來時對海灘的
附帶損害
更多了。
圖片只能説
話語讓它

不說的話
就像教皇
在筒倉中
而學詩的男孩
將他的以及她的
毫不費力
翻番。
是一個奔跑的
笨蛋，或者
說得更客氣一點
一個笨拙的命題。
你說你把
鉗子
放在哪裏？
她離宿命
只有這麼遠。
但他們只賣
單程票。
織物的經緯
被一陣陣包圍。
然後發生了
那個矩形被
陰影覆蓋。
只要你們
兩人溢出。

小拇指統治。
她是這樣
告訴我的。

文貞姬（南韓），詩人，東國大學講座教授，曾獲現代文學獎、素月詩歌獎、鄭芝溶文學獎、瑞典「蟬」國際文學獎等。2004 年詩集《噴泉》獲馬其頓泰托沃世界文學論壇年度詩人獎。2008 年獲韓國藝術評論家協會年度最優秀藝術家獎。曾參加美國愛荷華大學國際寫作計劃。英譯詩集有 *Windflower*、*Woman on the Terrace* 及 *I Must Be the Wind*。

Moon Chung-hee (South Korea) is a poet and Endowed Chair Professor at Dongguk University. She has won prestigious awards such as the Sowol Poetry Award, the Chong Chi-Yong Literature Prize, the Mogwol Literature Prize, and Sweden's Cikada Prize. She has participated in the International Writing Program at the University of Iowa. English editions of her books include *Windflower, Woman on the Terrace*, and *I Must Be the Wind*.

文貞姬

MOON CHUNG-HEE

中文翻譯：薛舟

English translation by Clare You, Richard Silberg, Seong Kon Kim, and Alec Gordon

화장을 하며

입술을 자주색으로 칠하고 나니
거울 속에 속국의 공주가 앉아 있다
내 작은 얼굴은 국제 자본의 각축장
거상들이 만든 허구의 드라마가
명실공히 그 절정을 이룬다
좁은 영토에 만국기 펄럭인다

금년 가을 유행색은 섹시브라운
샤넬이 지시하는 대로 볼연지를 칠하고
예쁜 여자의 신화 속에
스스로를 가두니
이만하면 음모는 제법 완성된 셈
가끔 소스라치며
자신 속의 노예를 깨우치지만
매혹의 인공향과 부드러운 색조가 만든
착시는 이미 저항을 잃은 지 오래다

시간을 손으로 막기 위해 육체란
이렇듯 슬픈 향을 찍어 발라야 하는 것일까
안간힘처럼 에스테 로더의 아이라이너로
검은 철책을 두르고
디오르 한 방울을 귀밑에 살짝 뿌려 마무리한 후
드디어 외출 준비를 마친 속국의 여자는
비극 배우처럼 서서히 몸을 일으킨다

化妝

把嘴唇塗成紫色
附屬國的公主坐在鏡子裏
我小小的臉蛋是國際資本的角逐場
巨商打造的虛構的電視劇
名副其實地達到了高潮
狹窄的領土上飄揚著萬國旗

今年秋天流行性感的棕色
按照夏奈爾的指示先擦胭脂
自我囚禁於
美麗女人的神話裏
如果到此為止，陰謀已算完成
偶爾毛骨悚然
意識到內心的奴隸
魅惑的人工香和柔和的色調
製造出錯覺，錯覺早已失去了抵抗

為了用手阻擋時間
肉體需要塗抹如此悲傷的香脂嗎
竭盡全力用雅詩蘭黛的眼線膏
圍上黑色的柵欄
在鬢角下輕輕噴一滴迪奧
終於做好外出準備的附屬國女人
像悲劇演員一樣緩緩起身

Putting on Makeup

Painting my lips scarlet,
I see in the mirror a vain princess, all made up—
my small face an array of international cities,
a theater where fictitious dramas
staged by cosmetic illusions converge,
a miniature territory where the flags of all nations lavishly flutter.

Sexy brown is the color à la mode this fall.
Putting rouge on my cheeks, as Chanel instructs,
adhering to the myth of a glamorous woman,
I see the conspiracy is almost complete.
Occasionally frightened by the slavery in my mind—
yet once again bewitched by the artificial perfume
that enchants, by the hallucination drawn in softly-toned colors—

my protest is only feeble and sporadic.
To stop the winged chariots of time
With Estee Lauder eyeliner, I carefully
Draw a dark border around my eyes
And dab a drop of Christian Dior behind my ears,
The colonized Femme elegante ready to sortie!
She makes her entrance slowly, like a tragic heroine.

(Translated by Seong Kon Kim and Alec Gordon)

공항에서 쓸 편지

여보 일 년만 나를 찾지 말아 주세요
나 지금 결혼 안식년 휴가 떠나요
그날 우리 둘이 나란히 서서
기쁠 때나 슬플 때나 함께하겠다고
혼인 서약을 한 후
여기까지 용케 잘 왔어요
사막에 오아시스가 있고
아니 오아시스가 사막을 가졌던가요
아무튼 우리는 그 안에다 잔뿌리를 내리고
가지들도 제법 무성히 키웠어요
하지만, 일년만 나를 찾지 말아 주세요
병사에게도 휴가가 있고
노동자에게도 휴식이 있잖아요
조용한 학자들조차도
재충전을 위해 안식년을 떠나듯이
이제 내가 나에게 안식년을 줍니다
여보, 일 년만 나를 찾지 말아 주세요
내가 나를 찾아가지고 올 테니까요

在機場寫信

親愛的，一年之內不要找我
我要去度假，婚姻安息年
那天我們倆並肩而立
無論喜悅悲傷都會不離不棄
宣誓結婚之後
一路走到今天
沙漠有綠洲
不，應該説是綠洲擁有沙漠
我們在裏面扎下鬚根
長出茂盛的枝葉
不過，一年之內不要找我
士兵都有假期
工人也會休假
甚至安靜的學者
也有為自己充電的安息年
現在我要給自己一個安息年
親愛的，一年之內不要找我
我會把自己找回來

A Letter from the Airport

Please, leave me alone for one year, my dear, my dear.
I'm on sabbatical from our marriage.
We've come a long way since our wedding vows
to stay together for better or for worse
until death do us part.
We settled at a desert oasis,
Rooted deeply and grew branches.
But please, for one year, don't try to follow me.
Soldiers needs to take leave.
A worker needs a holiday.
As quiet scholars go on sabbatical for replenishment,
I now take my well-earned leave.
So please don't' look for me for a year, my dear.
I'll return when I've found myself.

(Translated by Seong Kon Kim and Alec Gordon)

유방

윗옷 모두 벗기운 채
맨살로 차가운 기계를 끌어안는다
찌그러지는 유두 속으로
공포가 독한 에테르 냄새로 파고든다
패잔병처럼 두 팔 들고
맑은 달 속의 흑점을 찾아
유방암 사진을 찍는다
사춘기 때부터 레이스 헝겊 속에
꼭꼭 싸매 놓은 유방
누구에게나 있지만 항상
여장의 것만 문제가 되어
마치 수치스러운 과일이 달린 듯
깊이 숨겨 왔던 유방
우리의 어머니가 이를 통해
지혜와 사랑을 입에 넣어 주셨듯이
세상의 아이들을 키운 비옥한 대자연의 구릉
다행히 내게도 두 개나 있어 좋았지만
오랫동안 진정 나의 소유가 아니었다
사랑하는 남자의 것이었고
또 아기의 것이었으니까
하지만 나 지금 윗옷 모두 벗기운 채
맨살로 차가운 기계를 안고 서서
이 유방이 나의 것임을 뼈저리게 느낀다
맑은 달 속의 흑점을 찾아
축 늘어진 슬픈 유방을 촬영하며

乳房

上身全部脱光
赤裸裸地抱著冰冷的機器
恐懼散發著強烈的乙醚味
深入乾癟的乳頭
像殘兵敗將高舉雙手
尋找皎潔月光裏的黑點
拍攝乳腺癌照片
從青春期開始就被蕾絲布片
緊緊包裹的乳房
每個人都有
只有女人的乳房存在問題
像結了羞恥的果實
深深隱藏的乳房
我們的母親通過乳房
把愛和智慧送進我們嘴裏
這是大自然哺育世間孩子的肥沃丘陵
幸好我也有兩個
很久以來它們並不真正屬於我
而屬於我愛的男人
和我的孩子
但是此刻，我脱掉上衣
赤裸裸地抱著冰冷的機器
徹骨地感覺到這兩個乳房屬於我
尋找皎潔月光裏的黑點
拍攝低垂的悲傷的乳房

Breasts

Blouse and bra taken off,
I embrace the cold machine.
The strong anxious smell of ethylene
penetrates my crushed breasts.
Both arms raised like a defeated soldier,
I surrender to the mammogram
looking for a moon dark spot.
These breasts wrapped tight in lace
since my teens.
Though everyone has them
only women's are a problem;
like a sheaf of shameful confessions
breasts are kept a deep secret.
Our mothers fed us
wisdom and love though them
fertile hills of mammalian nature.
Fortunately I've owned two but
for a long time they were not mine;
they belonged to my lover
or to my babies.
Stripped now
Naked flesh embracing a machine
I own them to the depth of my bones.
These sad, drooping breasts,
clear moons being probed for dark spots.

(Translated by Clare You and Richard Silberg)

사랑해야 하는 이유

우리가 서로 사랑해야 하는 이유는
세상의 강물을 나눠 마시고
세상의 채소를 나누어 먹고
똑 같은 해와 달 아래
똑 같은 주름을 만들고 산다는 것이라네
우리가 서로 사랑해야 해야 하는
또 하나의 이유는
세상의 강가에서 똑같이
시간의 돌멩이를 던지며 운다는 것이라네
바람에 나뒹굴다가
서로 누군지도 모르는
나뭇잎이나 쇠똥구리 같은 것으로
똑같이 흩어지는 것이라네

愛的理由

我們必須相愛的理由
是共飲人世間的河水
同食人世間的蔬菜
又在相同的太陽和月亮之下
長出同樣的皺紋
我們必須相愛的
另一個理由
是我們在人間的河邊
拋出歲月的石子，哭泣
我們在風中翻滾
和素不相識的樹葉
或屎殼郎一樣
飄散

Why We Must Love

We must love each other
because we share the earth's water,
we share the vegetation of the earth.
Under the same sun and moon,
we all wrinkle and grow old.
And we should love each other
because we all cry while throwing time's stones
into the rivers of the earth
We tumble in the wind
without knowing one another.
Like falling leaves or scuttling beetles,
we are all separated and dispersed.

(Translated by Seong Kon Kim and Alec Gordon)

德米特里・維傑尼亞賓（俄羅斯），1959 年出生於莫斯科。畢業於外國語學院，現任教於莫斯科文藝與新聞學院。十七歲開始寫詩，已出版詩集六部。他的作品已被譯介到英國、美國、法國和德國。他曾獲得數個獎項，其中包括2004 年的皇冠獎，2010 年最佳詩集獎和2011 年紀念布羅茨基基金會的贊助獎。

Dmitry Vedenyapin (Russia) was born in Moscow in 1959 and started writing poetry when he was about seventeen years old. He has published six books of poems: *Protecting Veil* (1993), *Grass and Smoke* (2002), *Between the Cupboard and the Sky* (2009), *What Does the Sun Beam Mean* (2010), *Glass Laughs, Cigarette Sobs* (2015), and *Home Performances* (2015). His translations of poetry and prose (British, American, French and German classical and contemporary authors) have been published in various almanacs, anthologies, newspapers, books, and the magazine *Inostrannaya Literatura*. Vedenyapin won a few literary prizes including *Crown* (an annual award given by the Union of Moscow Writers for outstanding achievements in the field of literature) in 2004 and *Moscow Score* for the best poetry book in 2010. Vedenyapin is currently teaching poetry at the Institute of Literary Arts and Journalism. He also hosts a cultural program at the Pasternak Museum and lives in Moscow.

德米特里 · 維傑尼亞賓

DMITRY VEDENYAPIN

中文翻譯：汪劍釗

English translation by Yuri Vedenyapin

Упование сыроежки

...Рой мух на падали шуршал, как покрывало...
Шарль Бодлер «Падаль»,
пер. А.Гелескула

В насекомых тучах зудья-нытья
С кузовком по ельнику я кружился,
Весь в жуках да мухах, как будто я,
Невзначай скопытившись, разложился.

Перевод есть образ и знак потерь,
Грустный символ поствавилонской эры.
Пусть антропоморфно я был теперь
Бойкой иллюстрацией к стихам Бодлера.

Как в любых блужданиях последних лет
Поначалу казалось: спасения нет.
Но – хотя ни мох, ни тенёк, ни слизни
Не спасли вот этот конкретный гриб –
Повторяя просековый изгиб,
Промелькнула бабочка из прошлой жизни.

И сказал сыроежковый Иезекииль:
«Вот я видел, как в плоть облекается гниль,
В чащах правды под елками греясь»...

Над болотом яснела и хмурилась мгла,
Между кочек в чернике, краснея, росла
Сыроежка, лучась и надеясь.

紅菇的期望

……群蠅黑壓壓地圍著獸屍嗡嗡叫……
——波德萊爾《獸屍》

在瘙癢而酸疼的虱之烏雲中，
我挎著小筐在雲杉林裏轉悠，
全身落滿金龜子和蒼蠅，彷彿我，
偶然栽倒，在那裏自行腐爛。

翻譯是喪失之形像和標記，
是後巴比倫時代憂鬱的象徵。
而今，且讓我像一個人猿
成為波德萊爾詩歌大膽的插圖。

彷彿在近些年的迷途中，
最初似乎就是：不可拯救。
但是——哪怕苔蘚、陰影，哪怕蛞蝓
都不能拯救這朵具體的蘑菇——
蝴蝶卻從過去的生命
脫穎而出，重走林間彎曲的小路。

紅菇屬的先知以西結說道：
「我看見了肉體大面積的腐爛，
在雲杉之下真理的小樹林中烘烤……」
輕霧在沼澤上空顯露，皺起眉頭，
在草墩子裏，在越橘樹上，一朵紅菇
生長，泛紅，閃光並期盼。

The Faith of a Mushroom

A swarm of flies was rustling over the carcass like a blanket…
Charles Baudelaire's "Carrion"
(Russian transl. by A. Geleskul)

In the itchy whine of the insect swarms,
a small basket in hand, I wandered about the fir grove,
covered in bugs and flies, as if I,
having kicked the bucket, had decomposed.

Translation is an image and a sign of loss,
a sad symbol of the post-Babylonian era.
If only anthropomorphically, I had thus become
a vivid illustration for the poetry of Baudelaire.

As in all of the wanderings of the recent years,
it seemed at first: there is no hope.
And yet—even though neither the moss, nor the shade, nor the slugs,
could save this specific mushroom—
following the meandering forest path,
a butterfly from a past life flew by.

And thus spoke the Ezekiel of the mushrooms:
"And behold, the bones were once again covered with flesh,
warming themselves in the thicket of the truth under the fir trees…"
Over the marshes, darkness glimmered and frowned;
nestled among blueberry bushes was a blushing red
mushroom, beaming with hope.

Бабочка

Нельзя не признать,
что в последнее время
биология
в техническом отношении
шагнула далеко вперед.
Например, в распоряжении ученых,
изучающих бабочек,
сегодня имеются
крохотные радиопередатчики,
которые крепятся к тельцу насекомого
и нисколько–во всяком случае, по утверждению изобретателей–
не мешают полету.

Разумеется, в 60-е годы прошлого века
ни о чем подобном не могло быть и речи,
так что моему дяде энтомологу
приходилось по старинке
помечать свои «объекты»
обычной несмываемой краской.

Вдохновленный дядиным примером
я однажды поймал
залетевшую к нам на террасу
шоколадницу
и тоже пометил ее,
нарисовав у нее на спинке
корявую «А»,
начальную букву названия деревни,
где родители снимали дачу.

Согласно данным энтомологических исследований
шоколадницы живут до полугода
(с мая по октябрь)
и в отличие от других видов,
ведущих более или менее «оседлый» образ жизни,
свободно мигрируют
по всей Голарктике.
Однако «моя» бабочка
оказалась домоседкой.
Тем летом я видел ее
еще несколько раз:
на участке около дома
и снова на террасе:
присев на нашу марлевую занавеску,
она–как мне показалось–
дружески и чуть ли не заговорщицки
помигала мне
своими прекрасными темно-оранжевыми крыльями.

Вчера, сорок семь лет спустя,
в лесу, на пронизанной солнцем просеке
неподалеку от эстонской деревни Кясму,
за тысячу двести километров
от подмосковной Александровки
я опять встретил свою бабочку.
Конечно, она уже не та:
поседела и летает не так стремительно,
но ошибиться я не мог–
детскую кривобокую «А»
ни с чем не спутаешь.

Я не питаю иллюзий.
Нелепо было бы ожидать,
что хоть кто-нибудь
воспримет мои слова всерьез.
К тому же у меня нет доказательств.
Подозреваю, кстати, что даже
если бы доказательства
(скажем, фотографии)
существовали,
они все равно никого не убедили бы
просто потому,
что Такого Не Может Быть.

Между тем, это чистая правда,
только не обыденная,
ничтожная
и, по сути дела, никому не нужная,
а настоящая:
сияющая и неприступная,
такая,
в которую невозможно поверить.

蝴蝶

不能不承認，
最近一段時間
生物學
在技術層面
已向前走得很遠。
例如，在研究蝴蝶的
學者的控制下，
今天有一種
微型的無線電發射機，
它們被安放在昆蟲的身體上，
不論怎樣——任何情況，經過發明者的確認——
都不會影響飛行。

當然啦，在上個世紀六十年代，
這事兒根本就無法想像，
所以，我的昆蟲學家叔叔
不得不按照老規矩
用無法抹除的普通顏色
標注自己的「客體」。

叔叔的例子給了我靈感，
有一次我抓住
一名跳到我們陽台的女工，
做巧克力的女工，
我在她的背脊
描畫了一個拙劣的「A」，
村名的第一個字母，
父母在村裏租了一個別墅。

與生物學數據研究對應的是，
巧克力女工生活了半年
（從五月到十月），
有所區別的是，
或多或少過著一種定居的生活，
在整個泛北極區內
自由地遷移。
但是，「我的」蝴蝶
似乎不愛出門。
那年夏天，我
還見過它幾次：
在住宅附近，
在陽台上：
棲停在我們的紗簾上，
它——我覺得——
非常友善，彷彿一個小陰謀家
用它的翅膀，
美麗的深橙色的翅膀撲閃我幾下。

昨天，四十七年以後，
在森林裏，在陽光照徹的林間小道，
距離愛沙尼亞的愛斯基摩村不遠，
距離莫斯科郊外的亞歷山大村
有一千兩百公里，
我再次遇見了自己的蝴蝶。
當然，它已不是那一隻：
棲停和飛行也不是那麼敏捷，
但我不會弄錯——
我絕不會混淆
兒童時代歪斜的「A」。

我並不被幻覺所滋養。
期盼是荒誕的，
哪怕有人
鄭重其事接受我的話語。
對此我無法給予證明。
順便説一句，我甚至
懷疑是否有證明
（我們可能會説，有照片）
確實存在，
它們無論怎樣説服不了
任何人，
只是因為那樣的證明不存在。

其實，這是純粹的真理，
不過並非是日常的，
不值一提的，
本質上説，誰也不需要的，
卻是真實的：
閃光的和不可企及的，
那樣的，
人們不可能相信的真理。

The Butterfly

It must be acknowledged
that lately,
biology
from the point of view of technology,
has made great advances.
For example, scientists
studying butterflies
can these days use
tiny radio transmitters,
attached to the insect's body
and do not in any way, at least according to the inventors,
impede flight.

Of course, back in the 1960s,
something like this would've been completely inconceivable,
and so my uncle, an entomologist,
had no other choice but to do it the old way,
marking his "subjects"
with regular waterproof paint.

Inspired by my uncle's example,
I once caught
a small tortoiseshell,
which had flown onto our veranda,
and I, too, marked it,
by drawing on its back
a crooked "A,"
which was the first letter in the name of the village
where my parents were renting a dacha.

According to data from entomological studies,
small tortoiseshells can live for up to half a year
(from May to October)
and, unlike other species,
which lead more or less "settled" lives,
migrate freely
all over the Holarctic.
"My" butterfly, however,
turned out to be a homebody.
That summer I saw it
a few more times:
once in the backyard
and again on the veranda:
it sat down onto our cheesecloth curtain,
and, as it seemed to me,
good-naturedly and almost conspiratorially
winked at me
with its beautiful dark orange wings.

Yesterday, forty-seven years later,
in the forest, on a sunlit path,
not far from the Estonian village of Käsmu,
one thousand two hundred kilometers away
from Moscow Oblast's Aleksandrovka,
I once again met "my" butterfly.
Of course, it wasn't what it used to be:
it had gone gray, and it could no longer fly as swiftly,
but there could be no mistake—
a crooked childish "A"
is hard to confuse with anything else.

I am under no illusion,
it would be foolish of me
to expect anyone
to take my words seriously.
Besides, I don't have any proof.
I suspect, though, that even
if some form of proof
(for example, photographs)
existed,
it would still fail to convince anyone,
just because
This Cannot Be.

And yet it is the pure truth—
just not of the common
and insignificant kind,
which, frankly, is of no use to anyone,
but the real truth:
shining and unassailable,
the truth
which is impossible to believe.

哈里斯・武拉維亞諾斯（希臘），詩人、譯者、學者，1957年出生於羅馬，在布里斯托大學學習經濟學和哲學，在牛津大學（三一學院）取得哲學碩士和哲學博士學位。著有十二本詩集，其中*Vacation in Reality*（2009）獲Diavazo詩歌獎並入選希臘國家詩歌獎決選名單，另外*Sonnets of Despair*（2011）也入選過該獎項決選名單。他曾將但丁的《神曲》譯為希臘文出版。2005年2月，意大利總理親自為他頒發Cavaliere騎士名譽，意大利但丁學會亦頒發但丁獎，表彰他對意大利文化的貢獻。

Haris Vlavianos (Greece), born in Rome in 1957, is a prolific poet, translator and scholar. He studied Economics and Philosophy at the University of Bristol (B.Sc) and Politics, History and International Relations (M.Phil, D.Phil) at the University of Oxford (Trinity College). He has published twelve collections of poetry, including *Vacation in Reality* (2009), which won the prestigious "Diavazo" Poetry Prize and was short-listed for National Poetry Prize, and *Sonnets of Despair* (2011) which was also short-listed for the National Poetry Prize. For his contribution in promoting Italian literature and culture in Greece, the President of the Italian Republic bestowed upon him in February 2005 the title of "Cavaliere", while the Dante Society of Italy awarded him the "Dante Prize" for his publications on the *Divine Comedy*.

哈里斯・武拉維亞諾斯

HARIS VLAVIANOS

中文翻譯：錢穎超、關建容

English translation by David Connelly and Mina Karavanta

Η ΔΙΑΘΗΚΗ ΤΟΥ ΠΑΣΚΑΛ

Ακολουθώντας της Jorie Graham

I

Αργά-αργά το μάτι
μαθαίνει να φωτίζει το αόρατο,
ασκείται να βλέπει τα πράγματα
τη στιγμή που το νόημά τους δραπετεύει,
τη στιγμή που παραιτούμενα από την προσωρινή μορφή τους
χάνουν την (ιερή) αύρα της παρουσίας.

II

Λίγο πριν κλείσει τα μάτια
ζήτησε από την αδελφή του
να ράψει στη φόδρα του παλτού του,
(χωρίς καν να το κοιτάξει),
το σημείωμα που περιείχε
την «ακλόνητη απόδειξη
 της ύπαρξης του Θεού»,
βέβαιος πως μόλις τα ανοίξει
θ' αντικρίσει το φιλεύσπλαχνο,
 παντοδύναμο πρόσωπό Του.

III

Η παγερή μορφή του φιλοσόφου
αποτυπωμένη στο βλέμμα της αδελφής του,
(μπορούμε να φανταστούμε τη σκηνή,
τον χώρο όπου αυτή εκτυλίσσεται),
και το χαμένο – οριστικά πια –
περιεχόμενο της ύστατης σκέψης του.

IV

Η νύχτα που απλώθηκε αδιάφορα
πάνω στο άψυχο σώμα
ερμήνευσε σωστά
την τελευταία του επιθυμία:
όχι ως ανάγκη
ενός εγωτικού πιστού
να αποκρύψει την αλήθεια
που είχε λίγο πριν επινοήσει,
αλλά ως επιθυμία
να παραδώσει στους επερχόμενους
το κενό γράμμα
μιας μεγαλόπρεπης,
βαθιά ανθρώπινης, χειρονομίας.

V

Η αναπόφευκτη γνώση μιας νέας πραγματικότητας.
Και ο νους που τώρα αναπαύεται
(συμφιλιωμένος με την ατέρμονη μουσική των εννοιών)
μέσα στα αέρινα δημιουργήματά του.
Η δικαίωση του στοχαστή που μόνος,
χωρίς τις ευλογίες των πνευμάτων,
έφερε τον κόσμο στα μέτρα
του δικού του αφανισμού.

帕斯卡爾[1]的遺囑

擬喬瑞·格蘭瑟姆

I

慢慢地，眼睛
學會照亮那不可見的，
練習觀看事物
此時它們逃離了含義，
此時它們擺脫了臨時的形體
失去了存在的（神聖）光暈。

II

在瞑目前的瞬息
他請求姐姐
在外套襯裡縫上
（他連看一眼都來不及）
含有「上帝存在之
可靠證據」的
　　　　標記，
他確信睜開眼睛的時候
能看見祂[2]和藹
　　　　又全能的臉龐。

III

哲學家已經變冷的面孔
印在姐姐的眼裏，
（我們可以想像這個場景，
它所發生的地點），
以及那失卻的——永遠地——
臨終前的思緒。

IV

夜冷漠地跨越
他失去靈魂的身體
正確詮釋了
他的遺願：
並非需要
作為一個自私的信徒
隱瞞早些時候
發現的真相，
而是願意
向後來者們傳遞
一封空白的信
關於威嚴的、
極其人道的手勢。

1　譯註：帕斯卡爾（Blaise Pascal, 1623–1662）是法國數學家、物理學家和思想家，十七世紀最為重要的科學家之一。他提倡用科學實驗的方法發現真理，駁斥當時仍非常盛行的經院哲學的認識論，反對迷信古代作家。他晚年曾與耶穌會進行論戰，反對神權對思想領域的統治。但這不代表他不信仰上帝，他同時持有不可知論，認為理性是有限的。

2　譯註：指上帝。

V

對新現實的必然認知。
現在理智[3]安息
（它與概念紛繁的樂曲和解）
在他縹緲的作品裏。
思想者的辯護
不在於上帝的賜福，
他獨自一人
把世界帶入自身湮滅的尺度。

3 譯註：原文為nous，在哲學上常音譯為「努斯」。這個概念在不同場合使用時有不同含義，柏拉圖將其理解為「理性」，是人的最高認識或最高的認識能力，亞里士多德進一步區分「能動的理性」和「被動的理性」，並把這個術語用於神，認為神的活動是「關於思維的思維」或「思維自身的思維」。伊壁鳩魯把它理解為區別於感覺的一種認識活動。斯多葛派把「努斯」看作宇宙或邏各斯的表現，而新柏拉圖學派將這個概念推廣為理智世界。

Pascal's Will

Following Jorie Graham

I

The eye languidly
learns to illumine the invisible,
exerts itself to see things
the moment when their essence flees,
the moment when withdrawn from their temporary form
they lose the (holy) aura of presence.

II

Just before he closed his eyes
he asked his sister
to stitch inside his coat's lining,
(without even looking at it),
the note that contained
the "incontestable proof
of God's existence,"
convinced that upon opening them
he would see His merciful,
almighty face.

III

The glacial figure of the philosopher
impressed upon his sister's gaze,
(we can visualize the scene,

the space where it unravels),
and the forsaken—forever now—
content of its last-minute thought.

IV

The night casually spreading
on his lifeless body
has aptly interpreted
his last wish:
not as the need
of a self-centered believer
eager to disclose the truth
that he has just invented
but as the desire
to hand over to the progeny
the void letter
of a dignifying,
profoundly human gesture.

V

The inevitable knowledge of a new reality.
And the mind that now rests
(reconciled with the perpetual music of concepts)
inside its ethereal creations.

The vindication of the thinker that alone,
without the blessings of the specters,
has brought to the world the measures
of his own annihilation.

ΔΟΞΑΣΙΕΣ ΤΟΥ ΑΥΓΟΥΣΤΟΥ

I

Αν ένας άντρας στα σαράντα του
ζωγραφίζει ακόμη θάλασσες και περιστερεώνες,
αν στη σκέψη του καθρεφτίζεται
ένας ήλιος πιο καθαρός,
πιο σαφής, από τον ήλιο της πραγματικότητας,
αν η λέξη «Αμοργός» δεν είναι απλώς
το προσωπείο μιας φευγαλέας, εφηβικής ανάμνησης,
τότε ανάμεσα στο ποίημα της επιθυμίας
και το ποίημα της ανάγκης
ανασαίνει η αληθινή απώλεια.

II

Οι πρόλογοι εξαντλήθηκαν.
Δεν μπορούν να υποκαθιστούν διαρκώς το θέμα.
Πρέπει ν' αποφασίσει αν μπορεί
να κρατηθεί από αυτή την απόλυτη ιδέα
έστω κι αν έχει πάψει να πιστεύει στη δύναμή της.
Είναι ζήτημα πίστης πλέον.

III

Αλλεπάλληλες μεταμορφώσεις του παραδείσου.
Το μάτι προσπαθεί να ερμηνεύσει το αίνιγμα της ομορφιάς
καθώς στο βάθος ανατέλλει αργά-αργά η Δήλος.
Το καλοκαίρι μοιάζει αιώνιο.
Το ποίημα αρχίζει να επινοεί τον εαυτό του
τη στιγμή που εκείνος στρέφει το πρόσωπό του στο φως.
(Τη στιγμή που η φαντασία απελευθερωμένη
από τη συγκεκριμένη αίσθηση του διάπυρου λευκού
υψώνεται κάθετα στον ουρανό.)

IV

Ούτε ένα ιστιοφόρο στον ορίζοντα
να κόβει τον καμβά στα δύο.
Η εικόνα ενός δένδρου
με τα ανεμόδαρτα κλαδιά του να σαρώνουν το χώμα
δεν είναι σήμερα μέρος του σκηνικού.
Όμως η γριά που σέρνεται με τα γόνατα στην ανηφόρα
κρατώντας σφιχτά στο χέρι το εικόνισμά Της
είναι.

V

Ο άντρας βαδίζει μόνος στην παραλία.
Τον συγκινεί ακόμη ο μελωδικός ψίθυρος των κυμάτων,
ο τρόπος που το νερό νανουρίζει επίμονα τον βράχο.
Η φύση γύρω του
(αρμυρίκια, σάπιες ψαρόβαρκες, κροκάλες)
έχει μια μελαγχολική, ανεπιτήδευτη λαμπρότητα.
Αν ήταν να πεθάνει αυτή τη στιγμή
θα ήθελε να είναι εδώ
στον τόπο αυτό που έχει υπάρξει.
Έστω για λίγο.
Τώρα.

八月的信仰

I
如果一個男人到了四十歲
還在畫大海和鴿籠，
如果在他的腦海裏映照著
一輪太陽，比現實中的
更純淨，更清晰，
如果「阿莫格斯」[1]這個詞不僅僅是
易逝的青春記憶的面具，
那麼，在願望的詩
與現實的詩之間
喘息著的是真實的失去。

II
序言已經寫盡。
它們無法總是代替主題。
必須斷定
這樣絕對的理念是否可以掌控
直到它的力量失去信任的那一天。
這是個信念問題。

III
天堂的變幻接連不斷。
眼睛企圖解釋美的謎題
而提洛島[2]從海底慢慢升起。
夏日彷彿天長地久。
詩開始創作自己
此時他把臉轉向日光。

（此時，想像力重獲自由
從熾烈白色的具體感覺中，
垂直升上天空。）

IV
把畫布切成兩半的海平線上
一艘帆船也沒有。
畫中的一棵樹
狂風中亂舞的枝條掃過大地
這並不屬於今日場景。
而蹣跚上坡的老嫗
手裏緊緊攥著聖母小像
卻是。

V
男人獨自行走在海邊。
他仍感動於波濤低吟的旋律，

1 譯註：阿莫格斯（Amorgos）是希臘西南部的一個海島，屬於最重要的群島——基克拉迪群島。詩人在島上寫下了他的第一部詩集。另外，希臘著名詩人卡佐斯（Nikos Gkatsos）曾寫過題為《阿莫格斯島》（*Amorgos*, 1943）的長篇詩歌，為現代希臘超現實主義詩歌的名作。

2 譯註：提洛島是古希臘宗教、政治和商業中心，位於愛琴海上。根據神話傳說，女神勒托和主神宙斯相愛後有了身孕，遭到天后赫拉的嫉妒，赫拉下令禁止所有大陸和島嶼為她提供分娩之地。最後，提洛島從海中升起，成為浮島，宙斯將其固定，勒托最後在島上生下了太陽神阿波羅和月亮神阿爾忒彌斯。

和海水撫摸礁石的催眠曲。
他周圍的自然
（檉柳，朽船，卵石）
有一種哀傷的、天然的光彩。
要是此刻就死去，
他寧願就在這裏
在這個他曾存在的地方。
哪怕是片刻。
現在。

August Meditations

I

If a man in his forties
is still drawing seas and dovecotes
if in his thought is reflected
a sun more transparent,
more lucid than the sun of reality,
if the word "Amorgos" is not just
the mask of a fleeting, adolescent memory,
then between the poem of desire
and the poem of necessity
real loss is panting.

II

Prologues have been consumed.
They cannot always substitute the topic.
He must decide whether he can
hold on to this absolute idea
even if he has ceased to believe in its power.
It is a question of faith from now on.

III

Successive metamorphoses of paradise.
The eye tries to interpret the enigma of beauty
while Delos is slowly emerging in the horizon.
Summer feels like an eternity.
The poem begins to invent itself

at the moment when the man turns his face to the light.

(The moment when imagination
freed from the specific sensation of blazing light
vertically rises in the sky.)

IV
Not one sail in the horizon
tearing the canvas apart.
The image of a tree
with its wind-swept boughs scavenging the ground
is not a part of the scenery today.
Yet, the old lady creeping uphill on her knees
tightly holding Her icon is.

V
The man is walking on the beach alone.
He is still touched by the melodious whisper of the waves,
the way the water is persistently lulling the rock to sleep.
Nature around him
(cedars, rotten fishing boats, shingles)
has a melancholic, unaffected brightness.
If he were to die at this moment
he would want to be here
in this place where he has been.
Even for a while.
For now.

洛爾娜・克羅齊（加拿大）曾獲加拿大最負盛名的總督文學獎（詩歌）。她也是許多其他獎項的獲得者，包括三次獲得Pat Lowther年度最佳女性詩集獎，最近一次授予2016年的詩集《犯錯的貓》。由於對加拿大文學的貢獻，她還曾經五次被加拿大的大學授予榮譽博士稱號，包括蒙特利爾的麥吉爾大學。她是維多利亞大學名譽退休教授、加拿大皇家學會會員、官佐級加拿大勳章得主，已經出版了十七種詩集。她的詩歌被翻譯成多種語言，其中法語版和西班牙語版數量眾多。她在除了南極洲以外的各大洲都朗讀過詩。

Lorna Crozier (Canada) has received Canada's most prestigious literary award, the Governor General's Award for poetry. She has been the recipient of many others, including three Pat Lowther Awards for the best book of poetry by a Canadian woman, most recently in 2016 for a collection called *The Wrong Cat*. She has also been awarded five honourary doctorates from universities across Canada, including McGill University in Montreal, for her contribution to Canadian literature. A Professor Emeritus at the University of Victoria, a fellow of the Royal Society of Canada, and an Officer of the Order of Canada (the country's highest civilian honour), she has published 17 books of poetry. Her poems have been translated into several languages, including a book-length translation in French and another in Spanish, and she has read in every continent, except Antarctica.

洛爾娜 · 克羅齊

LORNA CROZIER

中文翻譯：梁小曼

From *The Sex Lives of Vegetables*

Lettuce

Raised for one thing
and one thing only,
lettuce is a courtesan
in her salad days.
Under her fancy crinolines
her narrow feet are bound.

選自《蔬菜的性生活》

萵苣

為一個目的而種植
僅僅一個目的，
在她的沙拉生涯裏
萵苣是個交際花。
在她華麗的襯裙下
細窄的腳已被綁

Onions

The onion loves the onion.
It hugs its many layers,
saying *O, O, O,*
each vowel smaller
than the last.

Some say it has no heart.
It doesn't need one.
It surrounds itself,
feels whole. Primordial.
First among vegetables.

If Eve had bitten it
instead of the apple,
how different Paradise.

洋葱

洋葱熱愛洋葱
它擁抱它層層外衣
念*O*，*O*，*O*
每個元音都小於
上一個

有人説它無心
它並不需要
它與自己為伍
感到完整，原始
蔬菜之初

假如夏娃咬了它
而不是蘋果
天堂將多麼不同

Cabbages

Long-living and slow,
content to dream in the sun,
heads tucked in, cabbages
ignore the caress of the
cabbage butterfly, the soft
sliding belly of the worm.

You know it's crazy
but they lie so still,
so self-contained, you imagine them
laying eggs
in the earth's dark pockets,
expect one morning they'll be gone,
dragging themselves
to the creek behind the house,

making their way
with great deliberation
to the sea.

甘藍

壽而遲緩
喜歡在太陽下做夢
頭埋起，甘藍
對白粉蝶的愛撫
無動於衷，青蟲
那滑動的軟腹

你知道這很奇怪
它們一動不動地躺著
如此克制，你想像
它們產卵在
大地黑色的口袋裏
某天清晨，它們將離開
費力地前往
屋後的小海灣

以巨大的從容
經那裏游向
大海

Potatoes

No one knows
what potatoes do.
Quiet and secretive
they stick together.
So many under one roof
there is talk of incest.

The pale, dumb faces,
the blank expressions.
Potato dumplings.
Potato pancakes.
Potato head.

In dark cellars
they reach across the potato bin
to hold one another
in their thin white arms.

馬鈴薯

沒有人知道
馬鈴薯是做甚麼的
安靜和低調
它們緊緊地挨著
一個屋檐下如此之多
已有亂倫的流言

蒼白，沉默的面孔
茫然的神情
馬鈴薯餃子
馬鈴薯薄餅
馬鈴薯頭

陰暗的地窖裏
穿過馬鈴薯箱子
它們瘦小蒼白的胳膊
相互擁抱

Cucumbers

Cucumbers hide
          in a leafy camouflage,
popping out
when you least expect
like flashers in the park.

The truth is,
they all have an anal
fixation. Watch it
when you bend to pick them.

黃瓜

黃瓜隱藏於
　　繁茂葉子的偽裝裏
在你意想不到時
冒了出來
像公園裏的探射燈

而真相是
它們都有著肛交
迷戀　留意看吧
當你彎腰去摘它們時

Peas

Peas never liked any of it.
They make you suffer for the sweet
burst of green in the mouth. Remember
the hours of shelling on the front steps,
the ping into the basin? Your mother
bribing you with lemonade to keep you there,
popping them open with your thumbs.

Your tongue finds them clitoral
as it slides up the pod.
Peas are not amused.
They have spent all of their lives
keeping their knees together.

豌豆

豌豆從沒喜歡過這事
它們在嘴裏破裂的
甜汁使人受不了，回想起
前門的台階上剝幾小時殼
那落入盆裏的咚咚聲？你的母親
拿檸檬汽水賄賂你，讓你待著
彈開它們，用你的拇指

你的舌頭滑過豆莢時
覺得它們就像陰蒂
豌豆並不愉悅
終其一生它們的
膝蓋都緊緊併攏

Carrots

Carrots are fucking
the earth. A permanent
erection, they push deeper
into the damp and dark.
All summer long
they try so hard to please.
Was it good for you,
was it good?

Perhaps because the earth won't answer
they keep on trying.
While you stroll through the garden
thinking *carrot cake,*
carrots and onions in beef stew,
carrot pudding with caramel sauce,
they are fucking their brains out
in the hottest part of the afternoon.

胡蘿蔔

胡蘿蔔在操
這大地。一個永恆的
勃起，他們往潮濕與
幽暗之地推得更深
整個夏天
他們如此費勁去取悅
你覺得好嗎？
好嗎？

或許是大地不應的緣故
他們推得更深
當你在花園裏散步
想著*胡蘿蔔蛋糕*
胡蘿蔔洋葱煮牛肉
胡蘿蔔焦糖布丁
他們則在最炎熱的下午
操得靈魂出竅

悠莉亞・費多奇克（波蘭），詩人、作家、譯者，現於華沙大學教授美國文學。她出版了五本詩集、一本短篇小説集，和兩部小説，作品已譯成十九種語言，其中包括一本關於詩歌與生態的三語詩集*Ekopoetyka / Ecopoética / Ecopoetics*。她的作品探索人類與自然關係，以至身份、他性和倫理責任等課題，是語言及環境研究協會會員。個人網站：www.ekopoetyka.com

Julia Fiedorczuk (Poland) is a poet, prose writer, translator, and lecturer in American literature at the University of Warsaw. She has published five books of poetry, a collection of short stories, and two novels (including the Nike-nominated *Nieważkość*). She is the author (with Gerardo Beltrán of a trilingual essay on poetry and ecology: *Ekopoetyka / Ecopoética / Ecopoetics*) and a member of ASLE (Association for the Study of Language and the Environment). In her writings she explores the relationships between human beings and non-human nature, as well as the questions of identity, otherness and ethical responsibility. Her work has been translated into 19 languages. Website: www.ekopoetyka.com

悠莉亞・費多奇克

JULIA FIEDORCZUK

中文翻譯：林蔚昀

English translation by Bill Johnston

Ramię Oriona

Wielkie poruszenie na tych gładkich morzach,
kłębią się ciężkie, ciemne ciała ryb.
To duch awaryjnie ląduje na wodzie,
ślizga się, tnie toń, wytraca prędkość, czas.

Czas rozdzielić poły słonecznego płaszcza,
uwolnić wiatr –

i już.

Pył międzygwiazdowy na listkach pierwszych drzew.
Rozmodlony zając strząsa słoną rosę,
lgnie do ciepłej ziemi wsłuchany w jej musujące tętno.

Asymilacja i dysymilacja. CO_2, H_2O,
i światło, światło, światło,
przemiana materii w materię, wzrost i dojrzewanie
w płaskim dysku falującej Galaktyki.

Czarna śmierć pulsuje cicho pomiędzy gwiazdami,
„Koło biegunu krąży wiecznymi obwody" –
płomienna Betelgeuse, Rigel, Bellatrix –
jadą Kosiarze na jesienne niebo, patrz!

Patrzymy. Masz we włosach mgłę i nitki pajęczyny,
niesiesz reklamówkę pełną zimnych gruszek.

獵戶臂

在平滑的海面出現了一場巨大的騷動，
四處佈滿魚群沉重、黑暗的身體。
那是緊急迫降在水面的幽靈，
它滑行，劃破深淵，減緩速度和時間。

是時候了，讓我們把陽光的衣襬分開，
讓風獲得自由——

好了。

星際之間的粉塵在第一批樹的葉片上。
虔誠禱告的野兔甩去帶有鹹味的露珠，
緊貼溫暖的大地，聆聽牠氣泡般的脈搏。

同化及異化。CO_2，H_2O，
以及光線，光線，光線，
在波動銀河的平盤上，
物質蛻變為物質，長大，成熟。

黑色的死亡靜靜地在星際間脈動，
「永恆地繞著北極運轉」——
閃亮的參宿四、參宿七、參宿五——
割稻人正行經秋天的天空，看！

我們抬頭仰望。你的髮間有霧和蜘蛛絲，
你手中提著一個塑膠袋，裝滿冰冷的梨。

Orion's Shoulder

Great turbulence on these smooth seas,
dark, heavy bodies of the fish are swirling:
the spirit is making an emergency landing,
cutting across the water, losing speed, losing time.

Time now to separate the tails of the sun's coat,
to free the wind—

it's done.

Interstellar dust on the young leaves of first trees.
A hare, rapt in prayer, brushes the salty dew
and presses to the warm earth, intent on its frothing pulse.

Assimilation and dissimilation. CO_2, H_2O,
and light, light, light,
metabolic conversion, growth and maturation
within the flat disk of the rippling Galaxy.

Dark death is throbbing softly among the stars,
"he turns about in a fixed place"—
fiery Betelgeuse, Rigel, Bellatrix—
the Reapers are riding through the autumn sky—just look!

We look. You've mist and strands of cobweb in your hair,
you're carrying a plastic bag full of cold pears.

Fort-Da

Sendeckiemu

śniło mi się, że byłam złym starcem, mówi
moja córka w piżamce koloru lobelii, kiedy
siedzimy przy stole jak portrety w sepii
poranka. kurz w moich oczach, a w jej

lśniących oczach puszyste anioły,
minotaury: „w życia wędrówce, na połowie
czasu" nie wiem, co dziecku powiedzieć
o krwi. w drodze do przedszkola

bawimy się, że jedna z nas nie żyje.

Warszawa, marzec 2009

Fort-Da

給山德茨基

我夢到，我是個邪惡的老人，
我女兒穿著半邊蓮色的睡衣，説。
我們坐在桌旁，在彷彿用褐色墨水
畫出的清晨中。在我眼裏有灰塵，而在她

閃亮的眼中則有著羽絨天使和
半人半牛的怪物：「我走過流浪人生的一半旅程」
我不知道，要怎麼對孩子
説血的事。在去幼兒園的路上

我們玩遊戲，假裝我們其中一人死了。

華沙，二零零九年三月

Fort-Da

for M. S.

I dreamt I was a wicked old man, says
my daughter in her lobelia-colored pajamas, as
we sit at the table like portraits in the sepia
of early morning. dust in my eyes, while in her

shining eyes are downy angels,
minotaurs: "on the path of life, half way
through our time" I don't know what to tell the child
about blood. on the way to pre-school

we play at one of us being dead.

Warsaw, March 2009

Wyjście

My, zarażeni, musimy stale ponawiać wezwanie.
Inaczej znikniemy.
Wchłonie nas ciemna noc jeży i mrówek.
Przerośniemy pleśnią.
I wsiąkniemy w grunt.

My, zarażeni, musimy stale ponawiać wezwanie.
Wpuszczać w siebie to zabójcze morze.
Bo trudno uwierzyć w pustkę, której nikt nie widzi.
Trudno nie szukać. Choćby po omacku.
Kimkolwiek jesteś, podaj mi swój głos.

Kimkolwiek jesteś, podaj mi swoje ciało języka
i dnia. Proszę, wyciągnij dłonie.
Dotknę cię lekko jak czas.

Kimkolwiek jesteś, podaj mi swoje ciało nocy.
Zliżę sól z twoich chłodnych powiek.

I zobaczysz świat.

My, zarażeni, musimy wszystko zaczynać od nowa.
Więc pozwól, że ukocham twój mrok.
Co w tobie rośnie, niech we mnie zakwita.
A owoce tych kwiatów niech ciebie nasycą.

Kimkolwiek jesteś,
biorę cię ze sobą.
Popatrz, tu jest droga.

A tu nie ma mapy.

Toronto, czerwiec 2009

出口

我們，這些感染者，必須不斷開始新的召喚。
否則我們就會消失。
刺蝟和螞蟻的黑夜會吞噬我們。
我們身上會長出黴菌。
然後滲入土壤。

我們，這些感染者，必須不斷開始新的召喚。
讓那致命的海洋進入我們。
因為你很難相信無人能見的虛空。
很難不去尋找。即使只能在黑暗中摸索。
無論你是誰，給我你的聲音。

無論你是誰，給我你舌頭和
白日的身體。請，伸出你的手。
我會輕柔地碰觸你，宛如時間。

無論你是誰，給我你夜晚的身體。
我會舔去你冰涼眼皮上的鹽。

然後你會看見世界。

我們，這些感染者，必須一切重頭開始。
所以允許我愛你的陰暗。
那在你體內成長的，就讓它在我裏面開花。
就讓那些花結出的果實解你的渴。

無論你是誰，
我會帶你上路。
你看，路就在此處。

而這裏沒有地圖。

多倫多，二零零九年六月

The Way Out

We the infected must constantly resume the challenge.
Otherwise we will disappear.
Be swallowed by the black night of hedgehogs and ants.
Be overgrown by mold.
Soak into the earth.

We the infected must constantly resume the challenge.
Admit into ourselves the killing sea.
For it's hard to believe in an emptiness no one can see.
It's hard not to seek. If only in the dark.
Whoever you are, give me your voice.

Whoever you are, pass me your body of tongue
and daylight. Please, reach out your hand.
I'll touch you lightly as time.

Whoever you are, pass me your body of night.
I'll lick the salt from your cold eyelids.

And you shall see the world.

We the infected must begin it all anew.
Then let me come to love your twilight.
What grows in you, may it bloom in me.
And may the fruit of those flowers sate your hunger.

Whoever you are
I take you with me.
Here is the road.

And look, there is no map.

Toronto, June 2009

Tlen

Pokażę ci miłość w jednej garści gwiazd.

Znasz feerię śniegu na przydrożnych liściach?
Fioletowy kontur grudniowego dnia?
Przyszłam tu, żeby oddychać.

Są mali tancerze w kropli rzecznej wody.
raje owadów za bramą ogrodu,
gniazdo w zgięciu ramion tamtej grubej sosny,
w gnieździe moich ramion mleczny oddech dziecka.

Lekko mieszkamy na wydechu świata,
jeden mrok dodany do drugiego mroku.
Usta przy policzku.
Policzek przy udzie.

Lekko mieszkamy na wydechu świata,
ciepła sierść wilczycy i jej ostre zęby,
brzytwa mrozu gładzi ciemną skórę rzeki,
jej mieszkańcy bezszelestnie opadają na dno.

Przyszłam tu, żeby oddychać.
Smutek naszych rzeczy na zimowym niebie.
Śnieg szybko topnieje na policzkach dziecka,
nasze oczy śmieją się do gwiazd,
niebo spotyka gładką skórę rzeki,
oddycham, oddycham więc jestem.

氧氣

我會用手裏的一把星讓你看到愛情。

你看過路邊樹葉上那多變的雪嗎？
還有十二月日子那紫色的輪廓？
我來這裏，是為了呼吸。

在每滴河水中有許多小小的舞者。
在花園門後有昆蟲的天堂，
在那棵大松樹的懷抱中有鳥巢，
而在我的懷抱築成的巢中，有孩子帶著奶味的呼吸。

我們輕盈地住在世界呼出的一口氣中，
一個黑暗被加進另一個黑暗。
嘴唇貼著臉頰。
臉頰貼著大腿。

我們輕盈地住在世界呼出的一口氣中，
母狼溫暖的皮毛和她尖利的牙齒，
嚴寒的剃刀溫柔地撫摸河流黑暗的皮膚，
她的居民無聲地遁入底層。

我來這裏，是為了呼吸。
我們俗務的憂鬱在冬日的天空中。
孩子臉上的雪迅速融化，
我們的眼睛向星星微笑，
天空遇見河流平滑的肌膚，
我在呼吸，我在呼吸於是我存在。

Oxygen

I'll show you love in a handful of stars

Have you seen the spectacle of snow on the roadside leaves?
The purple silhouette of a December day?
I came here in order to breathe.

There are small dancers in a droplet of river water.
Insect heavens beyond the garden gate,
a nest in the crook of the pine tree's broad arm,
in the nest of my arm a child's milky breath.

We dwell lightly at the outbreath of the world,
dusk heaped upon dusk.
Mouth next to cheek.
Cheek next to thigh.

We dwell lightly at the outbreath of the world,
the she-wolf's warm pelt and her pointed fangs,
the razor of ice that smoothes the river's dark skin,
its occupants sinking to the bottom.

I came here in order to breathe.
The sadness of our stories upon a winter sky.
Snow quickly melting on the cheeks of a child,
our eyes laughing with the stars,
the sky meeting the river's smooth skin;
I breathe, I breathe therefore I am.

平田俊子（日本），當代著名詩人、作家。生於島根縣，畢業於立命館大學文學部。1983 年獲得第一屆《現代詩手帖》「現代詩新人獎」後，引起詩壇關注。1984 年出版第一部詩集《報恩的薤》以來，相繼出版有《大西洋極樂世界裏的水鹽味淡！》、《同夜晚胖的女人》、《快活夫婦》、《信轉雨》、《現代詩文庫・平田俊子詩集》等詩集。其中詩集《終點站》獲得「晚翠詩歌獎」，《詩歌一星期》獲得「萩原朔太郎詩歌獎」。另外，還出版有多部小說集，其中《兩人乘坐》獲「野間文藝新人獎」，以及散文集《昨日的露珠》和戲劇集《走運的收音機》等。2016 年最新詩集《戲言的自由》獲得第26 屆紫式部文學獎。2003 年曾與詩人谷川俊太郎、作家高橋源一郎三人合出的《活在日語中》一書中，以每人創作一篇小說、一首詩和寫一個劇本之創意，給日本文壇帶來了不少新的刺激。她的詩歌作品「在讓故事性與詩歌的形式相抗衡的同時，以卓越的幽默感把潛伏在日常生活中的恐怖表面化」。1999 年在NHK 電視台舉辦的全國規模「詩歌拳擊」比賽中，以語言和即興詩作擊敗詩人白石嘉壽子獲勝而成為日本媒體一時關注的話題。

Hirata Toshiko (Japan) is a poet and novelist. During the 1980s, she, along with Hiromi Itō, emerged as one of the foremost voices so-called "women's boom" of poetry. Her poetry is known for its directness and black humor. *Tāminaru (Terminal)*, the 1997 anthology from which most of the poems translated here came, won the Doi Bansui Prize for poetry. She has also won the Hagiwara Sakutarō Prize for poetry for her 2004 collection *Shi nanoka (Poetry on the Seventh Day / Is This Poetry?)*. In recent years, she has increasingly turned to writing novels, which often feature ordinary people in bizarre circumstances that lead them to question the traditional family system and the spots allotted to them in society. Among her many novels are *Piano sando* (*Piano Sandwich*, 2001), *Futari nori* (*Two on Board*, 2004), which won the Noma Literary Prize for New Writers, and *Watashi no akakute yawarakana bubun* (My Soft, Red Place, 2007).

平田俊子

HIRATA TOSHIKO

中文翻譯：田原、鄧陽璐

English translation by Jeffrey Angles

私見、ゴッホの「寝室」

この部屋には二つの椅子がある
どちらも素朴な木の椅子だ
性別は　不明
年齢も　不明
二つの素材は不明だが
左の椅子は
右の椅子より大人びている
左が兄で　右が妹なのだろう

椅子と椅子の間にはテーブルがある
テーブルはやつれた顔をしている
椅子とテーブルの間に
恋愛関係はない
あるのは親子関係で
テーブルは椅子たちの母である

この部屋で一番目立つのはベッド
部屋の面積のほぼ半分を占めている
二つの椅子とテーブルをあわせたよりも
ベッドの体積ははるかに大きい
自分が巨漢であることを
ベッドは特に恥じてはいない

椅子とテーブルは立っているのに
ベッドは横たわっている
からだの具合が悪いのだ
「しっかりして　お父さん」
「しっかりして　あなた」
心配そうにベッドを見守る
妻と　二人の子供たち

夫はもう長くはないだろう
夫のからだを抜け出した血が
床を不吉な色に染めている
妻は水差しとコップを抱え
死に水を取る準備をしている

壁にかかった大きな布は
父の亡骸を覆うためのもの
それをするのは自分だと
兄はひそかに決めている

小さな妹は何もわからず
黙って父に寄り添っている

この絵を描いた画家は
後年　麦畑で自分を撃った
この絵を描いた画家は
生涯　家族に恵まれなかった

この部屋のベッドは
麦畑によく似た色をしている
この部屋の壁は
麦畑の上に広がる
空によく似た色をしている

觀梵高的「寢室」有感

這個房間有兩把椅子
都是樸素的木椅
性別不明
年齡不詳
兩把椅子的木材也無從所知
左邊的椅子
比右邊的椅子更像大人
左邊是哥哥，右邊是妹妹吧

椅子與椅子之間擺著桌子
桌子顯得愁容憔悴
椅子與桌子之間
不是戀愛關係
而是親子關係
桌子是椅子的母親

床在這個房間最醒目
佔據著房間一半的空間
兩把椅子和桌子合在一起
也沒有床的體積大
床沒有為自己是大漢
感到羞恥

椅子和桌子站立著
躺著的床
是身體出了毛病
「挺住啊，爸爸」
「堅強點啊，親愛的」
妻子和兩個孩子
彷彿擔心地照看著床

丈夫將不久於人世
從丈夫身體抽出的血
把地板染成不吉的顏色
妻子抱著水壺和杯子
準備著潤濕臨終者嘴唇的「死水」

牆上掛著一大塊布
是為了遮蓋父親的屍骨
這件事理應自己做
哥哥暗暗決定

年幼的妹妹甚麼都不知道
默默地靠著父親

畫這幅畫的畫家
幾年後在麥田開槍自殺
畫這幅畫的畫家
一生沒有受惠於家庭

這個房間的床
跟麥田的顏色很像
這個房間的牆
在麥田之上擴展
跟天空的顏色很像

Van Gogh's *Bedroom* as I See It

There are two chairs in this room
Both are simple, unsophisticated chairs
Their gender is unclear
Their age also unclear
Both of them are simple but
The chair on the left is a little more grown up
Than the one on the right
Maybe it is the older brother
And the one on the left the younger sister

There is a table between the chairs
The table wears a worn out expression
The chairs and table are not lovers
Their relationship is that of parent and child
The table is mother to the chairs

What stands out most is the bed
Which takes up nearly half the room
The bed's volume is greater than that
Of the table and both chairs put together
Still, the bed is not especially ashamed
About what a giant it is

The chair and table are standing
But the bed is lying down
It is not doing so well these days
"Get better, daddy"
"Get better, darling"
The wife and her two children
Watch over it with worried expressions

The husband doesn't have much longer
The blood that has drained from him
Has stained the floor an ominous color
The wife holds a pitcher and cup
Ready to carry water to her dying husband

The large piece of cloth hanging on the wall
Is to shroud the father's corpse when he dies
The older brother has already secretly decided
That will be his job when the time comes

Unaware of what is happening
His little sister crowds close to her father
But does not utter a word

The artist who painted this
Shot himself in a wheat field at the end of his life
The artist who painted this
Was not blessed with family while he was alive

The color of the bed in the room
So strongly resembles the color of wheat
While the walls of the room
So strongly resemble the color of the sky
Stretching over the field of wheat

ひ・と・び・と

あなたの声を聞かせてください
わたしの声を聞いてください

あなたの好きな窓を描いてください
わたしの好きな色にぬらせてください

あなたの湖をちょっと貸してください
わたしの山にのぼってもいいよ

あなたの鎖骨を見せてください
わたしのと片っぽ交換しましょう

あなたの運命線を見せてください
わたしの生命線を少しあげます

あなたの物語にさわらせてください
わたしの歴史を抱きしめてください

あなたの傷を見せてください
わたしの傷あとも見てください

あなたの泣き顔を見せてください
わたしも泣くからそばにいてほしい

あなたが生まれた町の
地図を描いてください
いつかいっしょに行けたらいいね

あなたの影を見せてください
わたしの影と並べてみましょう
きっとふたつはとてもよく似ている

あなたの名前を教えてください
わたしの名前も尋ねてください

人們

請讓我聽聽你的聲音
請聽聽我的聲音

請畫下你喜歡的窗口
讓我塗上我喜歡的顏色

請把你的湖泊借我一下
你也可以攀上我的山巒

請讓我看看你的鎖骨
跟我交換一根吧

請讓我看看你手上的命運線
我會給你一截兒我的生命線

請讓我觸摸你的故事
抱緊我的歷史

請讓我看看你的傷口
也請你看看我的傷痕

請讓看看你的哭容
因為我也哭泣，想讓你呆在我身旁

請畫出你出生的城市
甚麼時候能跟你一起去該有多好啊

請讓我看看你的影子
若與我的影子並肩
它們一定很相似

請告訴我你的名字
也請你問問我的名字

P-E-O-P-L-E

Please let me hear your voice
Please listen to my voice

Please draw a window you like
Please let me paint the color I like

Please lend me your lake
Feel free to climb my mountain

Please show me your collarbone
Let's exchange one of yours for mine

Please show me your line of fortune
I'll give you part of my life line

Please let me touch your narrative
Please embrace my history

Please show me your wounds
Please take a look at my scars

Please show me what you look like in tears
I also cry so I'd like you by my side

Please draw me a map
Of the town where you were born
Once day I'd like to go there with you

Please show me your shadow
Let's line yours up with mine
No doubt the two will look a lot alike

Please tell me your name
Please ask me my name as well

腕のない男

腕のない男が立っていた
吊り橋のような横断歩道をはさんで
わたしと男はむきあっていた
男の腕は二本ともなかった
信号が青になり男はやってくる
心配事があるふりをして
靴を見ながらわたしは歩いた
男とすれ違い
むこう岸について
橋を落としたあとでふりむき
男の古い上着を見た
上着の二本のからっぽの袖が
風になびくのをしばらく眺めた

腕はわたしが切ったのだ
余分な枝をはらうみたいに
鋸でギリリと切断した
ハンドルを握れないように
キーボードをたたけないように
ドアを開けて出ていかないように
女のところにいかないように
女の乳房をつかめないよう
女の首をしめられないよう
力いっぱい鋸を引いた
初めてにしては上手にできた
男も「うまい」とほめてくれた

腕を落とした男のからだは
冬の木のように簡潔になった
でも

腕は何度でもはえてくる
女の部屋にたどりつくころには
上着の二本のからっぽの袖は
枝のようなものでふくらんでいるのだ
胴体をまっぷたつに切ったところで
腕は何度でもはえてくるのだ

沒胳膊的男人

沒胳膊的男人站著
隔著像吊橋似的人行橫道
與我面對面
男人的兩條胳膊都沒了
綠燈亮後，他走過來
我裝作滿腹心事
一邊看著鞋子邁步
與他擦身而過
來到彼岸
在拆掉橋的痕跡上我轉過臉
對著穿舊上衣的男人
那兩隻空蕩蕩隨風飄動的
袖子眺望了很久

胳膊是我砍掉的
像除去多餘的枝條
嚓嚓嚓地用鋸拉斷
為了讓他握不住方向盤
為了讓他無法敲按鍵盤
為了不讓他開門外出
去找女人
為了讓他抓不住女人的乳房
和無法掐住女人的脖頸
我用盡全力拉動鋸子
雖為新手，我鋸得卻特別拿手
男人也一口稱讚我「老練」

掉了兩條胳膊的男人之軀
像冬天的樹木一樣簡單
不過

胳膊會無數次地長出來
在他好容易才走到女人的房間時
上衣上那空蕩蕩的兩隻袖子
鼓起了像枝條一樣的東西
即使把他的軀體鋸成兩截兒
胳膊還會無數次地長出來

Man Without Arms

A man was standing there without arms
He and I faced each other across the crosswalk
Suspended between us like a rope bridge
The man didn't have either of his arms
He walked this way when the light turned green
I looked at my shoes as I walked
Pretending to be worried
I walked by him
Once I had reached the other side
Once I had cut the bridge down, I turned to look
I looked at the man's old jacket
I watched as the two empty sleeves
Of his jacket fluttered in the wind

I was the one who cut off his arms
I amputated them with a saw
Like getting rid of two extra branches
So he couldn't hold the steering wheel
So he couldn't play the keyboard
So he couldn't open the door and go
So he couldn't go where she was
So he couldn't grab her breast
So he couldn't strangle her
I sawed with all my might
I did it well, considering it was my first time
Even he complimented me on my skill

The body of the armless man
Was as clean as a tree in winter
But

Arms grow back over and over again
When he reaches her room
The two empty sleeves of his jacket
Will have filled out like branches
Even when I split him clean in two
The arms grow back over and over again

宝物

世界で一番美しい言葉はコンセルトヘボウです

四年前のアムステルダム
午後のトラムにゆられていると
大きな建て物が前方に見えた
あれは何？　と尋ねると
コンセルトヘボウとあなたは答えた

コンセルトヘボウ
そのときの私には
それが何だかわからなかった
ただ　こうつぶやいたときの
あなたの声がとてもきれいで
以来この言葉は私の宝物になった

誰かがこの言葉を口にするのを
それまでも
そのあとも聞いたことはない
あなたがこの言葉をつぶやいたのも
あのときだけだ
ただ一度だけ耳にした言葉
私だけが聞いた
あのときの
あなたの
柔らかな
声

ここにこうして書いてしまうと
宝物はたちまち輝きを失い
蝉の死骸以下のものになる
大切なものを捨て去るために
私は秘密を打ち明けた
この言葉もあなたのことも
忘れるために

さよなら
私のコンセルトヘボウ
ときめくことはもうないでしょう
大切なものは何度でも
捨てなければなりません

別離がもたらすはずの甘い露さえ
ここに書くことで薄まってしまった
私は少しも傷ついていない
そのことを残念に思う

寶物

世上最優美的詞語是皇家音樂廳管弦樂團

四年前的阿姆斯特丹
坐在下午的電車裏搖搖晃晃
看見前方巨大的建築物
那是甚麼？我問
你回答那是皇家音樂廳管弦樂團

皇家音樂廳管弦樂團
對於這時的我來說
並不知道那是甚麼
只是　你輕言輕語的時候
聲音很美
之後這詞語就成了我的寶物

這之前
這之後　都再也沒聽過
誰再把這個詞語掛在嘴邊
你悄聲對我說這個詞語
也只有那個時候
僅此一次的耳語
只有我聽見
那時
你
溫柔的
聲音

這樣寫下來
寶物忽然就失去了它的光彩
連蟬的屍骸都不如
為了捨去這珍貴的東西
我説出了秘密
為了忘卻
這詞語和你

再見
我的皇家音樂廳管弦樂團
怦然心動的東西已經消失了吧
寶貴的東西必須要扔
很多次

甚至連本該別離帶來的甘露
也因這在這裏而變得淡了
我沒有受傷
只覺遺憾

Treasure

The most beautiful word in the world is Concertgebouw

Four years ago in Amsterdam
Shaken by the afternoon train
I spied a large building before us
What's that? I asked
The Concertgebouw, you answered

Concertgebouw
At the time I didn't know
What that meant
But when you whispered the word
Your voice was so lovely
That I have treasured it ever since

Until then I had never heard
Anyone utter that word
Nor have I since
The only time you whispered it
Was on that day
A word heard only once
That I alone heard
Your
Soft
Voice
That day

Writing it down like this
My treasure quickly loses its luster
Becoming less than a discarded cicada husk
I revealed this secret
To get rid of something dear
To forget both
You and that word

Goodbye
My Concertgebouw
My heart will never again beat quickly for you
One has to dispose of what is precious
Over and over again

Even the sweet dew of separation
Grows thin as I write about it here
I am not the least bit hurt
And that, I think, is
The most unfortunate part

馬卓爾・傑克遜（美國）著有四部詩集，包括*Roll Deep*（2015）、*Holding Company*（2010）、*Hoops*（2006）及*Leaving Saturn*（2002）。*Leaving Saturn*榮獲「科尼姆首部詩作獎」，並入選「全國書評人獎（詩歌）」。傑克遜屢獲殊榮，曾為美國普羅溫斯敦藝術作品中心、古根海姆基金、國家藝術基金會及哈佛大學拉德克利夫高等研究院的院士，並奪得普希卡獎及懷廷作家獎，更獲美國國會圖書館聯同陶友白基金會頒授皮尤藝術院士。他先後在多家大學任教，包括麻省大學（傑克・凱魯亞克駐校作家）、艾德菲大學、柏魯克學院（希德尼・哈曼駐校作家）、哥倫比亞大學及紐約大學。傑克遜現居於美國佛蒙特州南柏寧頓市，擔任佛蒙特大學「理查・丹尼斯綠與金」傑出教授，並為《哈佛評論》詩歌編輯。

Major Jackson (USA) is the author of four books of poetry including *Roll Deep* (2015), *Holding Company* (2010), *Hoops* (2006) and *Leaving Saturn* (2002), which won the Cave Canem Poetry Prize for a first book of poems and was a finalist for the National Book Critics Circle Award in Poetry. A recipient of a fellowships from the Fine Arts Work Center in Provincetown, Guggenheim Foundation, National Endowment for the Arts, and the Radcliffe Institute for Advanced Study at Harvard University, Major Jackson has been awarded a Pushcart Prize, a Whiting Writers' Award, and has been honored by the Pew Fellowship in the Arts and the Witter Bynner Foundation in conjunction with the Library of Congress. He has taught widely at the University of Massachusetts as the Jack Kerouac Writer-in-Residence, Adelphi University, Baruch College as the Sidney Harman Writer-in-Residence, Columbia University, and New York University. Major Jackson lives in South Burlington, Vermont, where he is the Richard Dennis Green and Gold University Distinguished Professor at the University of Vermont. He serves as the Poetry Editor of *The Harvard Review*.

馬卓爾 · 傑克遜

MAJOR JACKSON

中文翻譯：陳嘉恩、方梓勳

The View from Up Here

At sunset, winter mountains reach
across the page long as a look of love.
Sometimes my hands want
all of your syllables.
I walk in kindness
when you're around
which is to say I'm feeling Eastern.

I gather myself unto myself
because you hunger
for golden peaks.

The night horizon gently offers its diamonds
which we stash in silent mumblings.

When you speak, I feel unburied
yet hear still the dead of my own house.
No one cares that I count your eye blinks.
No one cares about all this hard water.
The hours are tall as polar caps,
and I quicken inside your name.

在這裏高處俯瞰

日落，冬日的山峰連綿
越過書頁，長長如愛的模樣。
有時候我的手想要
你所有的音節。
我走在好意中，
當你在左右，
就是説我感到東方的氣息。

我收集自己放進自己裏，
因為你渴求
金色的峰巒。

夜間地平線輕輕呈現它的鑽石，
我們收藏在默默的私語。

你説話時，我感覺沒有被埋葬，
但還聽到我房子的死寂。
沒有人理會我數算你眼睛的眨動。
沒有人理會這一切的硬水。
鐘點高高像極地冰冠，
而我在你的名字裏加速。

On Disappearing

I have not disappeared.
The boulevard is full of my steps. The sky is
full of my thinking. An archbishop
prays for my soul, even though
we met only once, and even then, he was
busy waving at a congregation.
The ticking clocks in Vermont sway

back and forth as though sweeping
up my eyes and my tattoos and my metaphors,
and what comes up are the great paragraphs
of dust, which also carry motes
of my existence. I have not disappeared.
My wife quivers inside a kiss.
My pulse was given to her many times,

in many countries. The chunks of bread we dip
in olive oil is communion with our ancestors,
who also have not disappeared. Their delicate songs
I wear on my eyelids. Their smiles have
given me freedom which is a crater
I keep falling in. When I bite into the two halves
of an orange whose cross-section resembles my lungs,
a delta of juices burst down my chin, and like magic,
makes me appear to those who think I've
disappeared. It's too bad war makes people
disappear like chess pieces, and that prisons
turn prisoners into movie endings. When I fade
into the mountains on a forest trail,
I still have not disappeared, even though its green façade
turns my arms and legs into branches of oak.
It is then I belong to a southerly wind,
which by now you have mistaken as me nodding back
and forth like a Hasid in prayer or a mother who has just
lost her son to gunfire in Detroit. I have not disappeared.

In my children, I see my bulging face
pressing further into the mysteries.

In a library in Tucson, on a plane above
Buenos Aires, on a field where nearby burns
a controlled fire, I am held by a professor,
a General, and a photographer.
One burns a finely wrapped cigar, then sniffs
the scented pages of my books, scouring
for the bitter smell of control.

I hold him in my mind like a chalice.
I have not disappeared. I swish the amber
hue of lager on my tongue and ponder the drilling
rigs in the Gulf of Alaska and all the oil-painted plovers.

When we talk about limits, we disappear.
In Jasper, TX you can disappear on a strip of gravel.

I am a life in sacred language.
Termites toil over a grave,
and my mind is a ravine of yesterdays.
At a glance from across the room, I wear
September on my face,
which is eternal, and does not disappear
even if you close your eyes once and for all
simultaneously like two coffins.

消失

我沒有消失，
林蔭大道滿是我的腳步。天空
滿是我的思維。大主教
為我的靈魂禱告，即使
我們只見過一次面，那時，他還要
忙著向會眾揮手。
佛蒙特州滴答作響的時鐘

往復的搖擺著，好像要向上拂掃
我的眼睛和我的紋身和我的隱喻，
跟著出現的是很多大段落的
灰塵，同時攜帶著我的存在的
微粒。我沒有消失
我的妻子在一個吻裏顫抖。
我把脈搏給了她很多次，

在許多國家。我們蘸在橄欖油裏的
一塊一塊的麵包是我們與祖先的交融，
他們也沒有消失。我把他們柔和的歌曲
穿戴在我的眼瞼上面。他們的笑容
給我自由，是我不斷跌進去的
火山口。當我咬著一個橙的
兩半，它們的橫截面好像我的肺，

果汁的三角洲在我的下巴爆發，像魔術一樣，
讓我在那些認為我已經消失了的人面前
出現。可惜太不好了，戰爭讓人們
就像棋子一樣消失，監獄
把囚犯變成電影的結局。當我消逝
於森林小徑的山上，
我仍然沒有消失，即使它綠色的表面
把我的胳膊和兩腿變成橡樹的樹枝。
那時我就屬於南風，
你此刻已誤會了，以為我往返的點頭
像一個哈西德哈派教徒在禱告，或者是一個在底特律
炮火之中剛剛失去兒子的母親。我沒有消失。

在我孩子們的臉上，我看到我隆起的臉龐
進一步壓進奧秘的深處。

在圖森的圖書館，在布宜諾斯艾利斯
上空的一架飛機裏，在附近燃著受控制的火的
田地，有人扶著我，是一位教授，
一位將軍和一位攝影師。
一位點著精心包紮的雪茄，然後逐頁嗅聞
我帶有香味的書，搜尋
苦澀的控制氣味。

我把他留住在腦海裏，像拿著一個聖杯。
我沒有消失。我咀嚼
拉格啤酒在舌頭上淡淡的琥珀色調，
沉思阿拉斯加海灣的鑽油台和所有油彩畫的鴴鳥。

當我們談論極限時，我們便會消失。
在德克薩斯州的傑士伯市，你可以消失在礫石地帶上。

我是神聖語言中的一條生命。
白蟻在墳墓上辛勞地工作，
我的頭腦是許多昨天的溝壑。
橫過房間一瞥，我把
九月掛在臉上，
這是永恆，不會消失
即使你最後一次閉上眼睛，
好像兩副棺木同時蓋上。

Picket Monsters

For I was born, too, in the stunted winter of History.
For I, too, desired the Lion's mouth split
& the world that is not ours, and the wounded children
set free to their turnstiles of wonder. I, too, have
blinked speechless at the valleys of corpses, wished
Scriabin's "Black Mass" in the Executioner's ear,
Ellington in the Interrogation Room.
I now seek gardens where bodies have their will,
where the self is a compass point given to the lost.
I call your name; the ground here is soft and broken.

糾察隊猛獸

因為我也在歷史中萎縮的冬天出生。
因為我也希望獅子的嘴巴咧開
和不是我們的世界，還有，受傷的孩子
獲得自由，可以去到他們奇蹟般的旋轉門。我也曾經
在滿是屍體的山谷眨了眨眼睛，說不出話來，希望
斯克里亞賓的〈黑色彌撒〉在劊子手的耳邊演奏，
艾靈頓在審訊室。
我現在尋找一所花園，在那裏面的身體都擁有自己的意志，
自我是迷途者的指南針。
我呼喚你的名字；這裏的土地面柔軟而破碎。

安雅・烏德勒（德國），1973 年生於施萬多夫，現往返於維也納、布拉格和雷根斯堡三地。她在維也納應用藝術大學教授詩歌，她的丈夫在布拉格，她的書在雷根斯堡。2003 年，她在雷根斯堡大學取得博士學位，研究題目為俄國現代主義詩歌。2003 年，詩集*münden – entzüngeln* 贏得 Leonce-und-Lena-Preis 詩歌獎。英譯詩集*engulf – enkindle* 入選2012 年最佳翻譯書獎決選名單。她最近的著作*ausgeübt. Eine Kurskorrektur* 探討與生態學有關的政治議題，該書獲得2014 年巴塞爾詩歌獎。2014 年，參加愛荷華大學國際寫作計劃。2015 年春天，在美國俄亥俄州歐柏林學院任駐校德語作家。烏德勒的詩集*brinnen*（2006）和*jana vermacht*（2009）都以書籍和聲音檔案兩種形式出版，後者更改變成裝置藝術展覽。

Anja Utler (Germany) was born in Schwandorf in 1973, and currently shuttles between Vienna, where she teaches poetry at the University of Applied Arts, Prague, where her husband lives, and Regensburg, where her books are. In 2003 she received her PhD at the University of Regensburg with a dissertation on Russian Modernist poetry. Her poetry collection *münden – entzüngeln* won the coveted "Leonce-und-Lena-Preis" for Poetry in 2003. The American translation by Kurt Beals, *engulf – enkindle*, was a Best Translated Book Award finalist in 2012. For her innovative poetic exploration of political issues such as ecology in her latest book *ausgeübt. Eine Kurskorrektur*, she was awarded with the "Basler Lyrikpreis" (Basel Poetry Prize) in 2014. She is Honorary Fellow of the International Writing Program of the University of Iowa (IWP '14), and in spring 2015, she was German Writer in Residence at Oberlin College, Ohio. Utler's works explore the impact of different media and modes of perception on the experience of a text: her works *brinnen* (2006) and *jana, vermacht* (2009) were both published in print and audio formats; *jana, vermacht* was also transformed into an installation for an exhibition. Poems by Anja Utler have been translated into numerous languages.

安雅．烏德勒

ANJA UTLER

中文翻譯：歐建梆
English translation by Kurt Beals

entgegen zu stehen:
eine verflechtung in neun teilen

I

ja, wieder und wieder ent-
wrungen sich, immer, bloß
bin murmeln bin: wie
versehrt werden, roh
unterm flimmerhaar,
roh

II

–vernehmen:
zerfurchen –

nur an den schürfstellen: ausgelöst
stehn, spüren, drifte schon: schlingre dir zu
durchs: zerklüftete höre – du sprichst mir vom
abraum, den halden vom: aufpflanzen,
windrose, -rad vom: rotieren sprichst, glänzendes
rotorblatt sagst du – es: schlingert, ja, schlingre, wie
arm, flügel pflügt: sich den rücken, ja, furcht
durch die erdrauch- die taubnesselfelder
und stumpft: erst am schulterblatt ab

III

– lösen: sich
eingraben –

wie ins wuchernde: einfinden wollen
sich: haspeln, entgegen, sich: auflegen,
-fiedern wie: werden zur: netzhaut
für furchen für flöze und: gänzlich sich
aufspinnen, netznervig werden so
zitternd ein: gitterblick – sehe du
ragst du sprichst – sein wie
hineingewirkt, -wunden: ins
nervenstrang dickicht aus taubnessel
erdrauch; ein pochen – vergesse –
ja höre, vernehme nicht mehr

IV

– entgegen:
entrinnen –

verspüre nur: taumle, ja, murmle – ein murmelnder
bachlauf, so heißt es – nicht kennen, ja
vielmehr: entgegen zu stürzen sich schließlich
zu: rinnen zu rieseln beginnen ergießen sich
sperrende kiefer bis: tief in die niederung
– talsohle, heißt es – wie: eingeschleust sein
aus dem: speichel- ins bachbett – ent-
lastungsgerinne – entsickert, gemündet in
schlingende flutende; fransen mäandernde
adern sich aus – richtung: talsperre – jochbein, ja
gurgeln und stockt stottert fängt: sich an reusen aus
hornblatt, gezähnt, flutet im: gerodeten mund

V

– stockung –

und dennoch: erinnere, nein ich vergesse nicht
teichwirtschaft heißt das ich sehe da hängen
gewässerstufen für karpfen-, forellenzucht aus-
gehoben den winter lang bleiben sie abgelassen
die ufer der schlamm sie starren sie: gleißen im frost
und ich stehe, natürlich, nicht lange dort

VI

– befallen:
sich kreuzen –

letztlich: gefallen sein, ja, wie
bestanden besiedelt die: mundhöhle
achsel vom: riedgras der luft über –
frostet, ja, starren – weiß: poche noch –
schon: scharen sporen sich im
geweiteten blick, und bloß: hingespreizt,
klaffe, die firnigen glieder beringt ja: vom reif
von der böschung gehöre schon, gleichsam,
verliere – nur poren mehr – und lieg mir fern

VII

– verweigern:
sich anschmiegen –

verharren noch und: will vergessen zu
sehen zu hören nur: murmeln mehr
vielmals am kiefer der wurzelstock,
fühlbar, der: schlamm in den poren
sie: schuppen sich schorfen – beginnendes
nesselfieber – die nässenden flerne sie
wollen gerinnen zu: rinde zu borke
im wind aus: nordost richtung murmle ich
landmasse tundra – versteppende haut
areale – sie: spreche ich speichle ich
mir in die schürfstellen, wunden, ziel:
lungenflechte statt haar

VIII

– fiebern: beher-
bergt sein –

regelrecht: luftmassen, vielmals hinweg
gefegt übers nässende (...) flügel –
schlägen gleich mitten: ins flimmerhaar,
bleiben, kaum regen sich: ausgeschabt
spröde, so dörrt selbst das: rippenfell,
federnd, von algenschicht rinde bespannt
überwuchert von krustenflechten mit
ihnen in: hungersymbiose – so heißt es –
zu bleiben, dürr aufgesteppt auf den
boden so: mehren sie sich brechen schon
unterm vogeltritt fingerschlag – vielteilig
werden – und krallen sich, staune, ins
bauchfell fest

IX

aufschrecken, schließlich und finde:
den kehlkopf entkernt ist
gehöhlt ihn: betasten die hände,
sie: nesteln, gefiedert, vom
brustkorb ab flechten sich
tiefer ins: schilf schlucken: licht,
gurgeln, dunkel ja, dämmrig
sie: stricken kielwärts ja kehlwärts
sich: hohlräume, mulden aus
halmen aus fingern aus (...)
gleichsam: den dommeln zu – nistplatz,
im singenden rohr heißt es – will wie
verfangen sein – treibgut – vernäht
werden bis in die: stimmritze raschle
fast zittre ich höre dich wieder: sagst
lied sagst du lied – was ist: lied

逆流而行：
連環九部曲

I

一而再，再而三彼此
鬆開彼此，總是坦蕩蕩的
喃喃細語：像是
受傷了，稚嫩地
在纖毛下
稚嫩地

II

——感知：　　只有在勘探途中：重獲自由
留痕——　　站立、感覺，一直飄流：向你
滾動：裂縫在傾聽——你訴説
一堆廢話，一灘渣滓：埋置、
羅盤——訴説輪盤：你説著滾動，閃爍的
它——旋葉：在轉動，正在滾動，如
手臂，如翅膀般犁著：它的背脊，留下車痕
透過地上的煙塵——透過垂死的鳥巢，
並直至：肩甲骨疲態初現

III

——掙脱：　　彷彿發瘋似的蔓延：如願出現
挖掘——　　在：疾風面前：散開，
如羽毛似地飄著：成長至：視網膜
為留下車痕為鑛層而生，並：全力
快速轉動，神經肌肉變得更發達，更
抖顫：從鐵窗中看出去——看到你
約隱約現，看到你在説話——彷彿
在盤問，在動怒：向著
地上的煙塵中，那神經纖維，那灌木叢裏
垂死的鳥巢；一聲敲打——忘記——
再也無法細聽細察

IV

——面向：逃脫—— 只要感覺：搖晃，或細語——那所謂的
潺潺溪流——不用認識，
只要：俯衝向下，直到
最後：細滴、細漏、傾盆似的落在
人煙罕至的松林，直至：深入下游處
——那人們所稱的波谷——彷彿是：偷偷
的：唾液朝河床洩出——流
走——滲出，流入
彎曲的水流，迂迴曲折的支流
邊緣——朝向：水壩——如頰骨般的水堤，
汩汩地流，跳動，結巴，並困住：陷進魚網的
金魚藻，齒狀的生物，淹沒在：那輪廓分明的嘴巴之中

V

——停滯—— 然而：我記得，不，我並未忘記
人們所稱為池塘漁業，我看到漂浮在
　　那裏的
水台，用作繁殖鯉魚，鮭魚
整個冬季牠們從岸邊
游至淤泥處，硬邦邦的：在寒霜下閃閃發光
至於我，當然無法長期在那裏佇立

VI

——降臨：
相遇——

最終：落下，就像是
大量聚集，並覆蓋在：口腔，
腋下的：結冰的莎草，極寒的
空氣，它們都僵住了——白茫茫中：仍然悸動的
孢子：成群擠滿在
遼闊的視野之中，純粹：目瞪口呆地
張開四散，那如環狀似的粗糙肢體：隨著
寒霜隨著各自所屬的堤岸，可謂，
失去——只有細孔——我從未曾想過

VII

——拒絕：
偎依——

仍然依舊：想要忘記
看過的聽過的，只要：多次
從根莖的頷骨中細語著，
清晰可見的：滿佈淤泥的
細孔：剝掉身上的苔蘚——初現的
痲疹——那疼得泣不成聲的瘡口
愈加渾圓：那外皮，那樹皮
在風中打轉，來自：東北大陸的苔原，
我細語著——那塊逐漸蔥郁的
高原——它們：我說著唾涎著
朝著勘探場，朝著傷口，朝著目標：
兜蘚而不是毛髮

VIII

——發燒：
躲避——

完全地：氣團多次的
擦過那泣不成聲的[…] 雙翼
隨即擺動：在纖毛裏
停留，幾乎靜止不動：被掏空了的
脆弱的，自我榨乾的：胸膜
在伸展著，並為一層層海藻所蓋著，
與殼狀地衣一同茂密地生長
在：人們所稱的——飢餓共生——
枯竭、被縫合
在土地上：它們自我繁殖，在
輕如羽毛的指尖下——形成
多邊形——並牢牢地抓住，目瞪口呆地
凝視著那腹膜壁

IX

最後變得驚愕，發現：
喉頭結去掉
給掏空：雙手輕觸，
它：摸索著，往那羽毛豐滿的
胸腔，深入那
纏繞不清的：蘆葦叢中，吞嚥：輕輕地，
咯咯地，在黑暗中，在薄暮中
它們：往外翻側往空心處插入
編織出：空間，（…）的如手指似的
一株株的波谷
也就是說：朝著麻鳽——築巢的地方，
在那人所稱為歌唱用的簧片——就像是
糾纏不清似地——零碎的殘骸——一針針的
給縫起來，直至：聲門噹啷作響
快要震動我再次聽到你：唸著
歌兒唸著歌兒——那首叫歌兒的歌兒

Counter Position:
An Interweavement in Nine Parts

I

again, then again came un-
wrung, apart, always, bare
am murmur am: as if
wounded, raw
under cilia,
raw

II

– perceive: just at the opencuts: set free
furrow – to stand, sense, to drift now am: pitching to you
through the: fissures hear – you speak of
waste heaps, of scree of: implanting, the
windrose, -wheel speak of: rotating, glistening
rotor blade you say – it: pitches, now, pitch, as a
veined arm, a wing plows: its back, engraves furrows
through earth-smoke through dead nettle fields
and at last: on the shoulder blade dulls down

III

– free from:
entreach –

as if wanting to enter: the wild growth
to: wind, towards, to: spread,
feather out as: to grow into: retina, network
for furrows for seams and: fully to
spin up, grow nervose so
trembling a: trammeled view – see how you
loom you speak – as if
worked-in, wound-in: to the
nerve-fiber thicket of dead, of deaf nettle of
earth-smoke; a throbbing – forget –
don't listen, perceive any more

IV

– encounter:
escape –

but feel only: stagger, well, murmur – a *murmuring*
stream, so it's called – not to know, just
to: plunge down toward finally
to: trickle to drip start to spill over
pinechoked till: deep in the lowland,
– the gullet, it's called – as if: sluiced
from the: spit- to the streambed – *run* –
off – exuded, poured out into
pitching flowing, meandering veins
fray – towards: waterstop – jugal dam,
gurgle and sticks stutters catches:
    on snares of
hornwort, toothed, flooding the: clearcut mouth

V

– stillstand –

and yet: remember, no i'm not forgetting
aquiculture it's called i see hanging there
watersteps carved out for carp, for trout
breeding sit drained out all winter
the shore the mud stiffen they: glisten in frost
and i, naturally, don't stand there long

VI

– befall:
cross –

at last: fallen, to be as if
colonized covered the: cavity, oral,
armpits frosted over with: reed grass with
air, so they, stiffen – white: throb still –
spores: already swarming the
wide-open eyes, only: gaping am
splayed out, the granular limbs so encircled: by frost
by the riverbank already fit, so to speak,
lose – just pores now – lie far from my mind

VII

– refuse:
nestle to –

remain still and: want to forget to
see to hear just: murmurs now
many times out from the mouth rootstock,
palpable: mud in the pores
they: scale off slough – a nettle rash,
nascent – the weeping sores
want to run thick turn: to rind turn to bark
in the wind from the: tundra i murmur
northeast landmass – skin patches turning
to steppe – they: speak i spit i
into my opencuts, wounds, goal:
lungwort for hair

VIII

– fever: find re-
fuge –

fully: air masses, frequently
swept across weeping (...) wing –
strokes straight: into the cilia,
stay, hardly moving: scraped out
so brittle, that even the: pleura dries,
pliant, coated in algae rind
grown thick with crustaceous lichens
in: hunger symbiosis with them
– so it's called – dry, stitched to the
ground: they multiply break from even
a featherweight fingerstroke – grow multi-
partite – and claw tight, am gaping, into the
abdominal wall

IX

finally, startled from sleep, find:
the larynx deseeded is
hollowed: hands palpate,
it: fumbling, feathered, from
ribcage entwine themselves
deeper into the: reed swallow: light,
gurgling, darkly well, dimly
they: keel towards hulls towards hollows
weave: cavities, gorges of
stalks of fingers of (...)
so to speak: towards the bittern – nesting place,
in the singing reed so it's called – grow
entangled as – flotsam and jetsam – stitched
up to the: glottis rustling
almost trembling i hear you again: say
song you say song – what is: song

陳滅（香港），原名陳智德，現任香港教育大學文學及文化學系副教授。2012 年獲選為參加美國愛荷華大學「國際寫作計劃」之香港作家。2014 年憑《地文誌：追憶香港地方與文學》獲第七屆香港書獎。2015 年獲香港藝術發展局頒發「香港藝術發展獎：年度藝術家獎（藝術評論）」。著有詩集《市場，去死吧》、《低保真》、《單聲道》及散文集《地文誌：追憶香港地方與文學》、《抗世詩話》等，另編有《香港文學大系1919–1949．新詩卷》等。

Chan Chi Tak (Hong Kong) is an associate professor in the Department of Literature and Cultural Studies at the Education University of Hong Kong. He represented Hong Kong at the International Writing Program at the University of Iowa in 2012; his essay collection, *Land and Words: Recollections on Places of Hong Kong and Its Literature*, received the Hong Kong Book Prize in 2014; and he was named 2015 Artist of the Year (Arts Criticism) by the Hong Kong Arts Development Council. His collections of poems include *Life in Mono* (2002), *Lo-fi Sound* (2004), and *To Hell with the Market* (2008).

陳滅

CHAN CHI TAK

English translation by Matt Turner and Weng Haiying

山雲我夢

列車載雲歸去，誰殘留心緒
喚眾多不耐煩的下班者儆醒？
影子殘留舊物我們腳踏不碎
只踏碎萬千喚不回的幻景

啼鳥常入我夢，山雲離我城遠去
驀見眾人形影不離共對的香港
殘缺人面如幻燈怕遇強光萎褪
不怕變幻只怕那「幻彩詠香江」

以幻彩泯滅香江的色彩，不自主
不覺察眾人勞苦憂患未了暗淚垂
紫荊花等待我們撫慰它好去入睡

白雲也詢問我們歸期但未有期
列車如再開行盼與我夢共馳騁
寄語燕雀遠飛前先啣去我們的影

I Dream of Mountains and Clouds

When the train carries clouds back, who remains in the mind
Calls all those getting off work and impatient to guard?
The remains of a shadow, the old things we stomp on but cannot break
Only break up thousands of illusions that can't be recalled

Singing birds enter my dreams, mountains and clouds leave my city and go far
Suddenly see, facing Hong Kong, the inseparable crowds
Broken up faces fear fading in the strong light, like film images
Unafraid of fluctuation, but afraid of a *Symphony of Lights*

The symphonic fades Hong Kong's color, no autonomy
No perception of the people's hardships and secret tears
Hong Kong's bauhinia waits for us to placate it to sleep

White clouds also ask us our return date, but there is none
If the train is starting again I hope it rides with my dreams
Send word to the finches to take our shadows before flying far

香港韶光

（一）
路燈初燃，我們不曉得它熄滅的時候
車燈復往照見旅者的倦意，且漸次融入
萬家泛黃或慘白參差的燈火
我們憑甚麼感官感應香港
香港也以同樣的燈光感應我們
我們無法感應的也許説不出的多

華燈亮起，因為感覺到人們熄滅
關閉語言，倦看海鏡浮沉的香港
歷史泛黃如瀕臨拆遷的家
轉眼改建像甚麼原是那幻彩詠香江！
我們瞠目結舌，又不受控地自發參加
為向旅客綻放只一瓣成分有毒的煙花

璀璨加璀璨，市民如夜蟲集結燈下
飛向堅固而灼熱的烏托邦
數字上升再偏軟，失落的目光仍舊流向
強迫性發動的幻彩詠香江
最後一班渡輪如霓虹下的魔術
變出鴿子、土地與兔女郎
只有水手看穿萬千重疊的樓宇
倚望底層暗燈殘照的海港

（二）
聽説海岸擴張到某程度就自行停步
它把擴張的任務留給了商場
我們用萎縮的海港填塞那購買海景的溝壑
用幻彩遮蔽那原本彩色的香江

情感如落花思念數不清的墮樓人
日暮，它把晚霞的責任留給家家戶戶
以亮燈代表一點僅餘的抵抗
誰人火葬，更換以信念擦亮的燈泡？
仍恐鈔票長翼如底片走了光
甚麼都別説，像一首K歌
我們的歷史總由別人代唱
唱不出的留給一台發光機器：
螢幕晃蕩如韶華飛絮的香港

璀璨加璀璨，數不清的離愁集結燈下
何處是列車奔赴終站的下一站？
市民列隊如公路停滯的車燈
巴士，沒有乘客的時候仍播放廣告
像每一個無法自主的乘客
以血汗、以無法不忍受的廣告
高唱給大廈無法休止的K歌
留下幻彩在台下偷偷暗換
打著呵欠悶了太累了的香江

Hong Kong Lights

1

The streetlamp turns on, and we don't know when it turns off
The headlights sway and light up the traveler's weariness, gradually merging into
All the homes' yellowing or pale blotched lights
By whatever sense that we sense Hong Kong
Hong Kong senses us with the same lights
And what we cannot sense is more than we can say

The colored lights light up, because it felt the people turned off
Shutting down language, wearily watching the ups and downs of Hong Kong reflect on the sea
History yellowing like a home on the brink of relocation
And in the blink of an eye the reconstruction is none other than a *Symphony of Lights*!
We're stupefied, but involuntarily participate
In order that the firework with the single toxic petal can blossom for the tourists

Brilliance on brilliance, citizens assemble under the lamp like nightbugs
Flying toward a solid and roasting utopia
Numbers go up, and then turn soft, the lost vision still flows toward
A forcefully launched *Symphony of Lights*
The last ferry like neon magic
Conjuring a pigeon: the land with the bunny assistant
Only sailors see through the thousands of overlapping buildings
Looking out at the dim light that barely illuminates the lower harbor

2

I heard the coast expands a certain degree and then stops
It leaves the task of expansion to the mall
We filled the gulf that bought the seascape with the shriveled harbor
And hide the original colors of Hong Kong in a mirage

Feelings like fallen flowers, longing for the innumerable suicides
Sunset leaves the task of its afterglow to all the householders
To use light to represent a bit of what remains of opposition
Whose cremation changes the lightbulb polished by faith?
Still afraid bills will grow wings like an over-exposed film negative
Don't say anything, like in karaoke
Our history's always sung by stand-ins
Songs we can't sing are left to a light-generating machine:
Screen flashing like in Hong Kong's "springtime"

Brilliance on brilliance, uncountable sad partings assembled under the lamp
Where's the next stop for the train rushing to the terminal?
The queue of citizens is like headlights at a standstill on the road
The bus still plays ads even without passengers
Like every passenger without their own will
With blood and sweat, with ads that must be endured
Loudly singing endless karaoke to the mansion
The mirage under the stage changes quietly
And Hong Kong is yawning and bored and so tired.

加鹽的咖啡

——紀念也斯先生

懷著中環老店自製的咖啡粉
你教巴士洋溢香味如雲彩
一刻的渴望和想像
總如燙熱咖啡
空氣中迅速冷卻
你用指頭在窗邊寫字
我讀到並仔細辨認

咖啡加鹽可以「墜火」
老婦的建議教你訝異
我們的舊郵局、舊車站
日常老街變奏奇幻世紀
即使歷史未記錄啼哭
也未能略去襤褸與壓抑
另有深刻語言仿似
一代人追隨探究的足跡

就在我所坐這巴士的前方
還是已落在後面？
已變遷的永追不回
但願我們有新想像
也許感覺怪異遠離既定口味
像一杯加鹽的咖啡

你已嚐過或許你也沒有？
我從不確知你的有和沒有
但知你嚐出的滋味與我的必不一樣
我忘了求問，加鹽的咖啡於你
或就是雲彩的味道
或就是雲彩的味道

Coffee with Salt

—in memoriam, Ye Si

Bundling off with homemade coffee grounds from an old shop in Central
You make the bus overflow with fragrance like clouds
A moment of yearning and imagining
like burning hot coffee
cooling down quickly in the air
You use a finger to write on the window's edge
I read it and identify it

Adding salt to coffee can "reduce internal heat"
The old lady's suggestion surprises you
Our old post office and train station
and plain old street fugue in this fantastic era
Although history lacks recordings of the crying
and wasn't able to omit the ragged and the depressed
the other incisive words are just like
the footprints a generation follows and studies

Right here in front of the bus that I'm sitting in
Or has it already fallen behind?
Can't keep on chasing after what has already changed
Hopefully we'll get a new imagination
Maybe it'll feel strange and far from our tastes
like a cup of coffee with salt

You've tasted it? Haven't you?
I never knew if you had or hadn't
But I always knew the flavors you and I tasted were not the same
I forgot to ask: was coffee with salt to you
the flavor of clouds
or the flavor of clouds

陳東東（中國大陸），祖籍江蘇吳江，在上海出生並長期生活。1980年代初在上海師範大學中文系讀書期間開始寫詩。主持編印過民間詩刊《作品》（1982–1984）、《傾向》（1988–1991）和《南方詩誌》（1992–1994）；自2005年以來參與策劃和組織每年一屆的「三月三詩會」，編選出版「三月三詩會」作品集三卷；另與詩人張耳合編了中英文雙語當代中國詩選《別處的集合：24人雙語詩選》（2007，紐約，Talisman House, 2007）。有詩集《夏之書·解禁書》（2010）、《導遊圖》（2013），詩文集《短篇·流水》（2000）和隨筆集《黑鏡子》（2014）、《隻言片語來自寫作》（2015）等十數種著作出版。現居深圳和上海專事寫作。

Chen Dongdong (Mainland China) was born in Shang-hai, where he has spent most of his life. He began writing poetry in 1980 while he was an undergraduate in the Chinese department at Shanghai Normal University, and he has been the editor of several unofficial literary journals, including *Works* (1982–1984), *Tendency* (1988–1991), and *Southern Poetry Journal* (1992–1994). Since 2005 he has been chief organizer of the Third of March Poetry Festival, publishing three volumes anthologizing the work. He co-edited *Another Kind of Nation: An Anthology of Contemporary Chinese Poetry* in English translation (Talisman House, 2007), with US-based poet Zhang Er. He has published over a dozen books of his own, including the poetry collections *Summer Book • Unbanned Book* (2010), *Tourist Map* (2013), and *Flowing Water* (prose poems, 2000), as well as the essay collections *Black Mirror* (2014) and *Words and Phrases from Writing* (2015). He now divides his time between Shanghai and Shenzhen.

陳東東

CHEN DONGDONG

English translation by Eleanor Goodman

導遊圖

餘輝佩戴著星形標記像一個錯誤。像一個錯誤嗎？
還沒有盡興的爬山新手們稍歇在四望峰，
聽下面雲動，滂沱一場雨。
他們要去的下一個景點更在天邊外。

*

大雨讓你和他只能在山前小旅館玩牌。
門窗敞開著，沒了生意的髮廊姐妹時時來探看。
霧氣群羊做得更出色——從桑拿浴室裏
湧進走廊，擠上雙人床；
雷霆鎮壓咩咩的叫喚聲。

*

藉著閃電，寫作者一瞥。
藉著閃電我記起履歷，更多旅程裏我被運送著，讀別的遊記：
藉著閃電有人從裏挾裏突出包圍圈，其中一個說「我已經濕了……」

*

攀登者決定把汗水流盡，
到金頂再把自己吹乾或曬乾。
他們後面的滑杆裏窩著舊樣版電影、烏雲和乳房：
匪營長的二姨太髮髻盤旋、盤旋向高海拔；
臭苦力腫肩，朝旗袍衩口裏回望落日淪陷進地峽。

*

這不是詩。是累活兒。
石匠花費了多少輪迴築成盤山梯？
新來者攀上新三岔口，觸摸深鑿進凹陷鷹眼和
夜之暈圈的青石路標：
抵達樂園還需花費多少輪迴呢？

*

但每一次回看像一座小樂園。
如果你打算把視線捆綁在叫不出名字的歸鳥腳杆上
回看得更遠，直至幽深……小樂園也許會翻轉為地獄。

*

一天的等待就已經漫長得讓人受不了。
新雨消滅舊雨，新希望成為記憶中振翅欲飛的舊幻想。
傍晚你和他終於厭倦了輸贏、反覆……
無聊牌戲幸好還可以變化小說：
——他打開檯燈……你讀《導遊圖》。

(2002)

Tourist Map

As if by mistake, the sunset is ornamented with the shape of stars. A mistake?
The hikers new to mountain climbing rest for a while on Lookout Peak,
listening to the cloud movement below, a torrential rain.
The next scenic spot they're heading to is beyond the horizon.

*

With the heavy rain, you and he stop in an inn by the mountain and play cards.
The windows and doors are open, and the idle salon girls come to watch.
A flock of sheep in the steam does even better—bursting out from the sauna's
shower room
into the hall, crowding onto the double beds;
the thunder overpowers their cries.

*

With the lightning, the writer catches a quick glimpse.
With the lightning I recall my résumé, other routes I've been sent on, other
travelogues I've read:
with the lightning a few people escape the obligatory circle, one of them says,
"I've already gotten wet… "

*

The climbers decide to sweat everything out,
they can sun or air themselves dry when they reach Golden Peak.
The bamboo sedan chairs behind them carry old reel films, dark clouds, and
breasts:
Commander Fei's concubine has coils of hair, spiraling to a high sea level;
The smelly porter's shoulders swell, facing the cheongsam's slits to watch as the
setting sun is captured by the isthmus.

*

This isn't poetry. This is heavy labor.
How many lives did the stonemasons spend building the steps that wind up
the mountain?
The newcomers climb to the new junction, touching the chiseled depression
of a hawk's eye
and the limestone road sign in the halo of night:
how many more lives will it take to reach paradise?

*

Yet each time we look back it seems like a little paradise.
If you plan to latch your line of sight onto the leg of a bird that cannot call its
own name
then look back farther, all the way into the depths… the little paradise may
turn over into hell.

*

A day's wait has stretched out so long it's unbearable.
New rain destroys old rain, new hope becomes a memory of an old fantasy
flapping its wings to fly.
In the evening you and he finally grow tired of winning
and losing, again and again…
At least the dull card games may still turn into a novel—
He turns on the reading lamp… you read *The Tourist Map*.

(2002)

奈良

往高松塚的路上如夢
櫻花樹下時時遇見花鹿
歇腳在一邊翻看雜誌克勞斯如是説

　　世界末日之際
　　我願正在隱居

坐到法隆寺殿的黃昏瞌睡唯美之迷醉
又有鐵鈴鐺叮叮
送來想像的斑鳩

　　走馬觀花一過
　　即為葬生之地

(2005)

Nara Prefecture

The path to Takamatsuzuka Tomb is like a dream
glimpses of spotted deer beneath cherry trees
stopping to rest and flipping through a magazine Klaus says

　　When doomsday comes
　　I want to be living as a hermit

Sitting in the dusk at Horyuji Temple and dozing off in aesthetic absorption
the little iron bells ding again
and bring imaginary turtledoves

　　We pass too quickly through
　　this place of birth and death

(2005)

譯自亡國的詩歌皇帝

擱下鋪張到窒息的大業：那接近完成的多米諾帝國
一時間朕只要一口足夠新鮮的空氣

*

而突然冒出的那個想法，難免不會被激怒貶損
——萬千重關山未必重於虛空裏最為虛空的啁啾

*

聲聲鳥鳴的終極之美更攪亂心
拂袖朕掀翻半輩子經營的骨牌迷樓

(2007)

The Emperor of Poetry Translates a Conquered Nation

Put aside the suffocating, grandiose enterprise:
  that nearly-completed domino empire
His Highness only needs one breath of fairly fresh air at a time

*

A sudden thought enrages him—
The many mountain ridges may be no heavier than the emptiness's
  emptiest chirps

*

The extreme beauty of the chirping is disturbing
Tossing his sleeve, His Highness topples the domino labyrinth he's
  managed half his lifetime

(2007)

莫名鎮

一條河在此轉折
　　　　　　　就已經造就了它
何況還有
兩岸水泥欄杆的粗陋

剝落綠色的郵政建築也足以
構成它
　　　再加上兩三棵樹
蔭陰裏停著大鋼圈自行車

小銀行則是必要的設施
玻璃門蒙塵，映現對街
蒙塵的學校
　　　　　廣播在廣播
廣播體操反覆的廣播

另一些影子屬　幾個人
不願意稍稍挪動自己
在橋上低頭看流水
在家庭旅館的橢圓形院子裏
看一盤殘棋浮出深井

百貨鋪。菜市場。剃頭店
網吧幽黯因為從前那是個穀倉
從電腦顯示屏顫抖的對話框

到來者跨出，來到了此地
他其實不想找在此要找的，正當
這麼個時刻……這麼個時代

(2010)

Unnamed Town

The bend here in the river
        has made it what it is
and even more so
the crudeness of the cement railings on both banks

The postal building with peeling green is enough to
form it
        along with two or three trees
under whose shade is a steel-wheeled bicycle

The small bank is a necessary facility
with glass doors covered in dust, setting off the dust-covered school across
  the street
        and the broadcaster broadcasting
a broadcast exercise routine on repeated broadcast

The other shadows belong to a few people
who don't want to move at all
on the bridge they look down into the river
and in the oval courtyard at their guesthouse
they watch a Go board emerge from a well

Convenience stores. Vegetable markets. Barbershops
an internet café dim because it once was a granary
and a visitor steps out
of the chat box on the computer screen, and arrives here
he doesn't want to find what he's looking for here, here in
this moment…this age

(2010)

陳先發（中國大陸），安徽桐城人。1989年畢業於復旦大學。著有詩集《春天的死亡之書》（1994）、《前世》（2005）、長篇小說《拉魂腔》（2006）、詩集《寫碑之心》（2011）、隨筆集《黑池壩筆記》（2014）、詩集《養鶴問題》（2015，台灣版）、《裂隙與巨眼》（2016）等。曾獲獎項有「十月詩歌獎」、「十月文學獎」、「1986年-2006年中國十大新銳詩人」、「2008年中國年度詩人」、「1998年至2008年中國十大影響力詩人」、「首屆中國海南詩歌雙年獎」、「首屆袁可嘉詩歌獎」、「天問詩歌獎」、「中國桂冠詩歌獎」、「2015年桃花潭國際詩會中國傑出詩人獎」、「陳子昂詩歌獎」、「安徽文學獎」等數十種。2015年與北島等十位詩人一起獲得中華書局等機構聯合評選的「新詩貢獻獎」。作品被譯成英、法、俄、西班牙、希臘等多種文字傳播。

Chen Xianfa (Mainland China) was born in 1967 in Anhui and graduated from Fudan University in Shanghai in 1989. He has published several books of poetry, including *Death in Springtime* (1994), *A Past Life* (2005), *The Heart of Writing Steles* (2011), *The Problem of Raising Cranes* (Taiwan, 2015), and *Crevice and Insight* (2016), as well as the novel *Soul-Stealing Opera* (2006) and the essays *Notes on Black Pond Dam* (2014). He has received well over a dozen domestic poetry prizes, including the October Poetry Prize, the 2008 Poet of the Year Award, and Fudan University's Award for Literary Achievement. His works have been translated into English, French, Russian, Spanish, and Greek.

陳先發

CHEN XIANFA

English translation by Tammy Ho Lai-Ming

前世

要逃，就乾脆逃到蝴蝶的體內去
不必再咬著牙，打翻父母的陰謀和藥汁
不必等到血都吐盡了。
要為敵，就乾脆與整個人類為敵。
他嘩地一下脫掉了蘸墨的青袍
脫掉了一層皮
脫掉了內心朝飛暮倦的長亭短亭。
脫掉了雲和水
這情節確實令人震悚：他如此輕易地
又脫掉了自己的骨頭！
我無限眷戀的最後一幕是：他們縱身一躍
在枝頭等了億年的蝴蝶渾身一顫
暗叫道：來了！
這一夜明月低於屋檐
碧溪潮生兩岸

只有一句尚未忘記
她忍住百感交集的淚水
把左翅朝下壓了壓，往前一伸
說：梁兄，請了
請了——

2004年6月2日

A Past Life

To escape, simply retreat into a butterfly's body
no need to clench your teeth or overturn parental plans and elixirs
no need to wait till you've spat out all your blood.
To make enemies, let it be against all humanity.
With a huff, he strips off his ink-stained robe
shedding his own skin
shedding his heart's dawn-dusk darting from long pavilions and short pavilions
shedding clouds and water
It *is* a shocking scene: so easily
he tears off his own bones again!
The final scene that lingers in my mind: they leap
and the butterflies waiting on the branch for a million years flutter their wings
quietly beckoning: Come!
This night the moon is lower than the eaves
Two shores grow out of the turquoise tide

Only one sentence is not forgotten
She withholds tears of a hundred emotions
presses down her left wing, then stretches forward
to say, Brother Liang, Farewell
Farewell—Farewell—

2 June 2004

從達摩到慧能的邏輯學研究

面壁者坐在一把尺子
和一堵牆
之間
他向哪邊移動一點，哪邊的木頭
就會裂開

（假設這尺子是相對的
又掉下來，很難開口）

為了破壁他生得醜
為了破壁他種下了
兩畦青菜

2005 年1 月

The Study of Logic from Dharma to Hui-Neng

Facing the wall he sits between a ruler
and a wall
in whichever direction he moves, the wood
splits

(Assuming that this ruler is relative
and falls, which is hard to say)

To break open the wall he was born ugly
to break open the wall he planted
two plots of vegetables

January 2005

街頭即繪

那令槐花開放的
也必令梨花開放

讓一個盲丐止步的
卻絕不會讓一個警察止步

道一聲精準多麼難
雖然盲丐
在街頭
會遭遇太多的蔑稱
而警察在這個國度，卻擁有
深淵般的權力

他們寂靜而
醒目
在灰濛濛的街道之間

正午
花香湧向何處不可知
懸崖將崩於誰手不可知

2016 年3 月

Improvised Street Painting

What makes pagodatree flowers blossom
Also makes pear flowers blossom

But what stays the steps of a blind beggar
Will never stop a policeman

How difficult it is to be precise
Although a blind beggar
On the street
will be scorned
The police in this country possess
Boundless power

They are silent
And smart
On these grey bleak streets

Noon
We know not where the flowers' fragrance blows
Nor do we know in whose hands the precipice shall crumble

March 2016

渺茫的本體

每一個緘默物體等著我們
剝離出幽閉其中的呼救聲
湖水說不
遂有漣漪
這遠非一個假設：當我
跑步至湖邊
湖水剛剛形成
當我攀至山頂，在磨得
皮開肉綻的鞋底
六和塔剛剛建成
在塔頂閑坐了幾分鐘
直射的光線讓人恍惚
這恍惚不可說
這一眼望去的水濁舟孤不可說
這一身遲來的大汗不可說
這芭蕉葉上的
漫長空白不可說
我的出現
像寧靜江面突然伸出一隻手
搖幾下就
永遠地消失了
這只手不可說
這由即興物象強制壓縮而成的
詩的身體不可說
一切語言盡可廢去，在
語言的無限彈性把我的
無數具身體從這一瞬間打撈出來的
生死兩茫茫不可說

2016年3月

The Unspeakable Body

Every silent object awaits us
Peeling itself from entrapped screams
The lakewater says no
Followed by the ripples
This is far more than an assumption: When I
Ran to the lake shore
Its water had just formed
When I climbed to the mountaintop, under the
Soles of my shoes that were completely torn
Liuhe Pagoda had just been built
Sitting idle on its top for a while
The light piercing the structure put me in a trance
A trance that's unspeakable
This lone boat on the turbid water is unspeakable
This latent body of sweat is unspeakable
The long emptiness
Above the banana leaves is unspeakable
My appearance
Is like a hand reaching out of a glass lake
Waving a few times
And disappearing forever
This hand cannot speak
These forcefully compressed improvisations of
Poems' bodies do not say
All languages are obsolete—in
The infinite elasticity of the language let my
Countless bodies be salvaged in this instant
From between life and death's unspeakable shores

March 2016

不可多得的容器

我書房中的容器
都是空的
幾個小缽，以前種過水仙花
有過璀璨片刻
但它們統統被清空了
我在書房不捨晝夜的寫作
跟這種空
有甚麼樣關係？
精研眼前的事物和那
不可見的恆河水
總是貌似刁鑽、晦澀——
難以作答。
我的寫作和這窗縫中逼過來的
碧雲天，有甚麼樣關係？
多數時刻
我一無所繫地抵案而眠

2016 年 1 月

Rare Containers

The containers in my library
Are all empty
Several small pots had been for daffodils
Which had blossomed for a while
But they are all emptied out
I write day and night in this library
What is the relationship between me
And this emptiness?
My careful study of the things before me and
that Ganges River, cannot be seen,
always seem difficult, obscure—
difficult to answer.
And what is the relationship between my writing
And the blue sky squeezed through the crevices of the windows?
Occasionally
leaning on the desk, associated with nothing, I sleep

January 2016

香港國際詩歌之夜 2017
International Poetry Nights in Hong Kong 2017

主辦單位 Organizers

香港中文大學文學院
Faculty of Arts, The Chinese University of Hong Kong

香港詩歌節基金會有限公司
Hong Kong Poetry Festival Foundation Limited

協辦單位 Co-organizers

香港中文大學中國文化研究所
Institute of Chinese Studies, The Chinese University of Hong Kong

香港中文大學出版社
The Chinese University Press

香港大學美術博物館
The University Museum and Art Gallery, The University of Hong Kong

香港大學文學院
Faculty of Arts, The University of Hong Kong

香港科技大學賽馬會高等研究院
Jockey Club Institute for Advanced Study, Hong Kong University of Science and Technology

香港科技大學人文學部
Division of Humanities, Hong Kong University of Science and Technology

廣州時刻文化傳播有限公司
Moment Communications

活字文化
MoveableType Legacy (Beijing) Co., Ltd.

當當
DANGDANG

贊助 Sponsors

中國會 The China Club

北京匡時國際拍賣有限公司 Beijing Council International Auction Co., Ltd.

先鋒公益基金會 UCF Charity Foundation Limited

卓爾書店 the zall bookstore

斑馬谷文化發展有限公司 Zebra Valley Culture Development

馮鑫牟希文夫婦 Feng Xin (Larry) and Mu Xi Wen (Maggie)

蓮華書院 Lianhua Academy